Wild Blackberries

Wild Blackberries

Recipes and memories from a New Zealand table

ROSIE BELTON

Foreword by Margaret Mahy

Published by Allen & Unwin in 2014

Allen & Unwin
Sydney, Melbourne, Auckland, London

83 Alexander Street
Crows Nest NSW 2065
Australia
Phone:　(61 2) 8425 0100
Fax:　　(61 2) 9906 2218
Email:　info@allenandunwin.com
Web:　　www.allenandunwin.com

Cataloguing-in-Publication details are available
from the National Library of Australia
trove.nla.gov.au

ISBN 978 1 87750 533 1

Set in 11/14 pt Adobe Caslon Pro by Bookhouse, Sydney
Printed and bound in Australia by Griffin Press

10 9 8 7 6 5 4 3 2 1

MIX
Paper from
responsible sources
FSC® C009448

The paper in this book is FSC® certified.
FSC® promotes environmentally responsible,
socially beneficial and economically viable
management of the world's forests.

*To all who want to eat and live well, and who find joy
in the creating and sharing of food.*

For Mark who has journeyed with me;

*Our children and their partners
who joined us along the way;*

*And to the grandchildren, hoping you
will carry on the tradition.*

Contents

Foreword

*Like a lot of other people I love food, I always
have loved it, and am sure I always will.*

There have been times when I struggled to cook well, read recipe books carefully and tried hard to be accurate when measuring ingredients, so it came as a shock to me when one of my daughters looked at me critically across her dinner plate.

'How is it, everyone's dinner tastes nicer than ours?' she asked me.

The words are burned into my memory to this very day.

Everyone needs to eat and most of us love eating. We all know that food is a fundamental human need and it reaches us in a great variety of ways. We vary food according to the time of day, we experiment with it (working out what we like best). We decorate it. And finally we consume it. We chew it, taste it, swallow it and digest.

A book like this one by Rosie Belton exemplifies our love of food . . . the mystery and romance of it, beyond mere nutritional

requirements. It is an exploration of one individual's relationship to food, and of the emotional satisfaction and inspiration food can provide. But it is an account both personal and universal. As Rosie writes about her individual journey and insights (reinforcing them with various recipes) she can spark off memories in her readers of separate magical experiences in which connections with food have been made.

I remember that, many years ago, I went to London to meet the American entrepreneur and editor who had ushered my books into the children's book markets of the world. I left behind me a New Zealand which, in those days, could only boast of a rather naïve, possibly primitive cuisine. Arriving in London I was taken to join my editor, who was staying at the Savoy Hotel surrounded by a grandeur I had never previously encountered. In due course we went to the dining room to have a meal. I will never forget my first mouthfuls of the entrée. Don't misunderstand me! I had enjoyed many meals in New Zealand but I had never tasted anything quite so commanding yet subtle as that entrée at the London Savoy. They must have employed a particularly able cook. As I say, it was many years ago and I cannot remember just what it was I was eating, but I do remember that moment of transforming taste—the revelation of what richness there could be in wonderfully prepared food.

Rosie's complex involvement with food is deep seated, springing initially from childhood memories of a grandmother who was a lively and generous hostess, regularly entertaining large groups of people, all exuding pleasure at being together, eating well and having a good time. So Rosie remembers not only the delicious

food, but its social variety and impact—the lively debates and flow of pleasurable emotions that it engendered.

She did not herself begin cooking at all seriously until she was twenty and just married, but the impact of those early days lingered on, colouring—and flavouring—what is too often regarded as a somewhat banal activity. Of course the New Zealand of today is very different from what it was when I left it to make that first trip to London.

Food is now celebrated in various subtle ways, and we can confidently expect from it variety and often deep pleasure. During the 1970s people became involved in the self-sufficiency movement, started baking their own bread, or even making their own cheeses. And over the next decade eating out or taking advantage of someone else's good cooking became increasingly popular. Food preparation grew beyond being a skill. It became an art, and in this book Rosie writes not only as a cook, but as an artist, invoking images of colour, texture and smell, while acknowledging the emotional power that simple eating can have for human beings—and quite possibly for other species as well. Some of the themes Rosie touches on seem detached from cooking as it is commonly understood, and yet, for Rosie, inspiration is not confined to the kitchen. The world around her . . . the environment in Governors Bay where she lives . . . the rocky hills against the sky, the long Lyttelton Harbour that stretches out in front of us, all help to establish a mood, an inspiring series of imaginative contexts for the preparation and enjoyment of food. Her accounts of cooking acknowledge personal connections, moods and insights that are not commonly seen as flowing into the cooking process.

So finally, this book is not simply a good cooking book (which it is) but a great, and in many ways unexpected pleasure, to read in all sorts of ways. Read on! Cook on! Eat on! Be part of a universal human need, experience and art.

Margaret Mahy

Preface

The preparation of food—the smells and tastes and textures—have accompanied me throughout the journeys of my life. Looking back over the years, very often food memories have become the marker posts defining boundaries, demarcating challenges and change.

Perhaps it is idolatry—sometimes it feels like pure wickedness to love the tastes, textures and aromas so much. In times of joy food has enhanced the feeling of celebration and in times of sadness it has provided colour and comfort. And in times of anxiety and emptiness its preparation gives rhythm and meaning to the day and offering food to others brings a sense of accomplishment and fulfilment. When all else fails—cook!

Rosie Belton

CHAPTER 1

Childhood down-under

I remember my mother, a dutiful and perfectionist New Zealand housewife, for her cooking. She perfected the Kiwi gastronomy of the 1950s and 60s, turning out three meals a day—it was before eating out became common. Her pavlova, the classic special-occasion dessert dish of our childhood, was hard on the outside but soft and slightly chewy on the inside. This plateau of meringue we saw as a symbol of our Kiwiness (although the dessert's provenance is hotly contested by our trans-Tasman neighbours).

Sol's pavlova

Here is my daughter-in-law's adaptation of my mother's recipe.

8 egg whites
550g caster sugar
1 tbspn cornflour
1 tspn balsamic vinegar
½ tspn rose water

1 Preheat the oven to 180°C. Line a baking tray with baking paper.

2 Beat the egg whites until stiff.

3 Add the sugar, a little at a time, and continue beating for 20 minutes or until the mixture is shiny and stiff.

4 Carefully fold the cornflour, balsamic vinegar and rose water into the beaten egg whites and sugar.

5 Use a spatula to spoon the mixture into a 23cm circle, taking care to avoid any air bubbles. (While the meringue looks small at this stage, it will almost double in size as it cooks.)

6 Put the tray in the oven and immediately turn the temperature down to 150°C and bake for one hour.

7 After an hour, turn the oven off and leave the pavlova in the oven as it cools for a further 30 minutes.

If not using the pavlova straightaway, cool and store in an airtight container.

SERVES 8–10

Brandy snaps were English treats made from a mixture of butter, golden syrup, sugar and flour, flavoured with powdered ginger. The brandy, if indeed it was ever there, seems to have disappeared over the years. I remember my mother carefully shaping the still-warm soft lace-like biscuits around a scrubbed broomstick and leaving them to cool to form tubes. When cool and crisp, they were filled with whipped cream, which had been flavoured with vanilla and sweetened with sugar. You bit into the crisp tube and had to be careful to avoid dropping blobs of cream on your best dress—it was a wonderful experience.

I also remember plates of butterfly cakes, their upturned wings sprinkled with icing sugar, and sponge cakes, light and fluffy as promised on the baking powder packet. When the tea trolley was loaded with these delicacies and my mother had dressed in her floral best, she was ready to greet afternoon tea guests.

Roast beef emerged at lunchtime on Sundays, accompanied by Yorkshire puddings, and we ate the golden delicacies with great delight as they soaked up the rich brown gravy surrounding the beef.

Yorkshire pudding

This was an unquestioned part of our English heritage, consumed with the Sunday roast. It can cook while the meat rests and the gravy is made.

6 tbspn flour
2 eggs
milk, approximately 200ml
salt

1 Put the flour in a bowl and make a well in the centre.
2 Drop in the eggs and stir, gradually adding milk until the texture is thick as cream. Beat well.
3 Pour into a preheated dish or greased muffin tray with a little hot butter and bake in the oven for 10 minutes.

SERVES 6 (MAKES 12 SMALL PUDDINGS)

The Sunday roast would often be followed by a pudding, usually fruit sponge made with cooked Golden Queen peaches, Black Doris plums or apples. It's a very filling dessert, especially good for cold weather.

Fruit sponge pudding

The spongy sweet topping is now a favourite with my grandchildren. This works with most fruit, but the favourites in this household are plum and apple. Serve it with cream, yoghurt or ice cream, or all three.

100g butter
½ cup sugar
2 eggs
2 cups plain flour
2 tspn baking powder
pinch of salt
1 cup milk
4 cups stewed fruit

1　Preheat the oven to 160°C.
2　Soften the butter and sugar together and beat in the eggs. Add the sifted flour, baking powder and salt in three lots, alternating with the milk. Beat until smooth after each addition.
3　In a baking dish, place the stewed fruit.
4　Pour the topping mixture over the fruit until there is an even coverage.
5　Bake for 20 to 30 minutes, until cooked. (When testing, a skewer should come out clean.)

SERVES 6–8

Porridge with cream and brown sugar was the offering from our dad in the mornings. Oatmeal porridge, cooked well, smooth on the plate and warm in the stomach, was our winter breakfast staple.

Other favourites in my mother's repertoire included Gregg's instant puddings. Just a pint of cold milk and sweet, powdery flavoured stuff from a packet, which you would beat up with the hand-held egg beater. Like magic, it would set in minutes. It came in a variety of flavours, including chocolate, which is the one I remember most.

And the Gregg's fruit cordials that came in exciting colours for children—lime green, bright orange and cherry red—and were mixed with pounds of sugar into an appealing syrupy cordial. Not surprisingly, school dental clinics in the 1950s did a roaring trade.

My brother and sister and I had two homes feeding us; the other belonged to our maternal grandmother, who lived just down the road. With her adherence to old values and tastes and her love of gathering people around the table, it was in Gran's kitchen I learnt about bread-making and apple dumplings and we collected fresh eggs from her back yard. Chickens later arrived in our back yard as well, but ours were white chooks—Gran's were black and speckled, and ranged free in the sheep paddock outside her kitchen.

At Gran's I also learnt about animal husbandry—that turkeys sat on eggs from which chicks hatched, that sheep dogs produced puppies and horses foaled.

My earliest memories of my Gran and Fuffa's horses were the big Clydesdales in the bottom paddock, still being used for ploughing (as a child 'Fuffa' was my word for Grandfather, and he remained Fuffa for all the family for the rest of his life). I also remember the major annual harvest of vegetables, flowers and fruit. From the orchard, both my mother and grandmother made jam and bottled all kinds of fruit to preserve the taste of summer and to help the family budget.

Mum's tomato sauce was a favourite, the colour and texture so different from the thick, dull red ketchup in a squirty plastic bottle that we all later came to accept.

Mum's tomato sauce

Well, actually, this is my sister-in-law Anne's version of Mum's recipe. It won't disappoint—it makes a nice red sauce and, if you double the ingredients, makes a good quantity. Once tried, you won't want to buy ketchup again. I collect tomato passata bottles and have 6 warming in the oven ready to bottle the sauce.

3kg tomatoes, cut into chunks
550g onions, chopped
900g sugar
30g salt
350ml malt vinegar
40g whole spice berries or pickling spice mix, tied in a muslin square

1 Put all ingredients into a large preserving pan and boil for 3 hours or until it has reduced by one-third. Stir occasionally to make sure it doesn't catch on the saucepan.
2 Remove muslin with pickling spice.
3 Cool and put through a Mouli or sieve.
4 Reheat to simmering before bottling into hot clean bottles.

MAKES APPROXIMATELY 4.5 LITRES.

The relationship between growing things, keeping farm animals and keeping a good table to satisfy the appetite was bedded in early and unconsciously. This awareness of the strong link between labouring in the garden, pride in growing food and preparing and eating that food also came from my father's side of the family. There weren't many areas of connection for me with my paternal grandparents, but food was one of them. From them I learnt all about apples, onions, carrots and the home-spun wisdom that went with them—an apple a day keeps the doctor away and carrots make you see in the dark. Onions, well, they make your hair curly, don't they?

No thought was given in the early 1950s to the fact that individuals may have different sensitivities and reactions to food. All that mattered was putting flesh on the bones, pinkness in the cheeks and energy in the gait. At that time in New Zealand, the Truby King and post-war baby-boom babies were being grown like cabbages. There was free health care, free dental care in schools, government subsidised housing and free and compulsory school milk supplied by the well-meaning leaders of the day.

It was at my maternal grandmother's I first learnt to drink weak tea with no milk. She didn't like milk except when she used it in her cooking. Maybe too many years spent dairy farming meant that the smell of the milk put her off—it was a great relief to me that I didn't have to have milk at her place. My mother also disliked milk and milk products but not to the same extent. I don't recall how I avoided those dreaded quarter pints of milk at school morning tea that were forced upon children, but I know I would have found a way to get rid of the contents of that bottle.

Then there were the apples, stored in the cool outside my brother's bedroom window. Granny Smiths, bright green with dew droplets shimmering on their perfect skins, and Red Delicious, Golden Delicious and Cox's Orange. My father and his father treasured them all. It was part of the ritual of our daily life to reach out of my brother's bedroom window for another apple during the night. The memory of the taste of those apples drives me to continue planting heritage apples in my house orchard.

I can't remember an exact time or date when food, including its tastes, textures and smells, first became a passion for me. Maybe being passionate, in general, was a way of being for me from an early age. The long table in the dining room at my grandparents' was the site of many a heated debate, political and otherwise, and many delicious meals. And there was always a pudding, usually made with home-grown fruit—apple dumplings were a particular favourite.

Apple dumplings

Finding this recipe after many years brings back happy memories of after school treats at my gran's. We ate these warm for pudding and cold the next day, after school, from where they sat on a plate in the 'safe'—the cool cupboard that was where Gran stored food that needed to be kept cool before she had a fridge.

For the pastry
150g plain flour
½ tspn salt
pinch of sugar
1 tspn baking powder
120g butter, cut into small pieces
4–4½ tbspn cold water

For the apples

6 Granny Smith or other cooking apples, cored and peeled
6 tspn butter (1 tspn per apple)
¾ cup brown sugar
1 tspn cinnamon
½ tspn ground nutmeg

For the sauce

3 cups water
2 cups white sugar
1 tspn vanilla extract
4 tbspn butter

1 Heat the oven to 200°C. Butter a large baking dish.

For the pastry

2 Place the dry ingredients into a bowl and add the chopped cold butter.
3 Rub the butter into the flour using the tips of your fingers to ensure the breaking up of the butter and then add the water. Continue to work the mixture until you have achieved a pliable dough.
4 Roll out the pastry and cut into six square pieces, each big enough to enclose one of the apples.
5 Place a whole apple in the centre of each square of pastry.
6 Cut the butter into six pieces and insert a piece into the opening of each apple.
7 Divide the sugar between the apples, and spoon at least one teaspoonful into the cavity of each apple.
8 Sprinkle the cinnamon and nutmeg over each apple.
9 Bring the pastry up and around each apple, making sure the dough completely covers each one and is sealed well at the top, and place them in the baking dish.

10 For the sauce, place the ingredients in a saucepan and bring to the boil, simmering for 5 minutes until all the sugar is dissolved. Pour over the dumplings.

11 Put into the oven and bake for 50 to 60 minutes.

12 Serve warm with cream or ice cream.

SERVES 6

CHAPTER 2

The times, they are a changin'

The 1960s had arrived—they were times of change as the wider world was beginning to re-enter the New Zealand consciousness. First it came creeping in through music and fashion, bringing new faces to our place—faces from overseas, people with different eating habits and different expectations. We were young and keen to take on the world. The alcoholic drinks available to us, as young teens, were mostly spirits stolen from parents who didn't bother to lock their alcohol cabinets, apple cider and Asti Spumante.

For the first time, you could buy yoghurt. That first yoghurt was a sensation in late-1960s Nelson. It was mixed with local boysenberries—not raw as we were used to eating, but slightly heated with syrup and then bottled and poured over the yoghurt. This was a hit with us. And there was coffee using real coffee beans, not instant powder. Suddenly there were coffee houses and cafés, like 'Chez Eelco'.

The coffee culture was born. Nelson, our small quiet town in the north of the South Island, renowned for its sunshine hours, became a breeding ground for new ideas, artistic experiment and exploration of new ways. Food was part of this and so Chez Eelco, fondly called 'the Chez' or 'the House of Eelco', named after its founder and owner Eelco Boswijk, a Dutchman remembered for his character, became a place where the young enthusiasts of life would gather to share ideas, taste new food, listen to new music, make music, and fall in love.

European immigrants were bringing new options to our diets and education to our palates. We tasted our first olive oils. And salami . . . well, that was just fantastic. It was our first taste of the world outside. We flocked in during the heady times of the 1960s to have our senses awakened.

There were fruit salads with large pieces of all varieties of fresh fruit, so unlike the finely diced cooked fruit we had at home. There were salad dressings that weren't made with sweetened condensed milk, malt vinegar and mustard—they were made with new ingredients, olive oil and balsamic vinegar.

French vinaigrette

Here's my favourite vinaigrette recipe. I keep a bottle on the kitchen shelf at all times.

⅔ cup olive oil
⅓ cup balsamic vinegar
2 crushed garlic cloves
2 tbspn honey (I use clover)
1 tspn mustard (choose your favourite)
salt to taste

1 Place all the ingredients in a screw-top jar or clip-top bottle and shake. Taste and adjust seasoning and the proportions of oil and vinegar if required.

MAKES 300ML

I still sometimes have a yearning for the creamy salad dressing made with sweetened condensed milk from my childhood, so here's that recipe as well.

Condensed milk salad dressing

Stored in the fridge, this will keep indefinitely.

4 tbspn vinegar
1 tbspn sugar
1 tspn salt
1 tspn tspn dried mustard powder
1 × 400g can sweetened condensed milk

1 Mix all the ingredients except the condensed milk together.
2 Gradually add the condensed milk, stirring to combine.

MAKES 2 CUPS

Later in the 1960s and into the 70s, 'flower power' hippie influences began to arrive in New Zealand, bringing a new social–political movement and experimentation with every aspect of life. Like so many others in our cultural milieu, we changed our diet and became vegetarian, celebrating pulses and vegetables. Some of us learnt how to grind our own wheat for bread-making and how to make soft cheeses from the goats we grazed. We grew vegetables, spray free of course, and organic, although the term wasn't used during that era. We just were organic gardeners, using compost and animal manure to enrich the soil. We juiced our organically grown apples and kept chickens for free-range eggs.

We celebrated our return to a more natural lifestyle. Some became so committed to that lifestyle that they became almost fanatical. Others merged their awareness with aspirations for study and professional career development, as my husband and I did. We fed many mouths during the 1970s, always more than our immediate family—fellow travellers, fellow adventurers, and fellow idealists. Many of us developed homes beside plots of land that supplied food to the household. It was not an easy path, rearing small children, studying and trying to maintain the 'good life' as we passionately followed our goal of changing the world for the better. We thought it was new, but it was the way our grandparents and great-grandparents—true pioneers—had lived, without the 'back up' we had.

Food co-ops appeared and these supplemented what we grew in our gardens. Vegetables and fruits for the week came neatly arranged in cardboard boxes. The contents were organic, hand picked and carefully packed ready for pick-up or delivery. We began buying staples, such as rice, sugar and flour, by the sack, enough to last for months.

And bread . . . well, we learnt to make it again, as our grandmothers and great-grandmothers had before us. For most of us, our mothers had seen it as an unnecessary task as they shopped at the corner dairy for their fluffy white loaves. We were rebelling against this refinement of flour and sugar, this greater reliance on staple food items purchased from the local dairy.

We wanted to feel secure, knowing we could fend for ourselves. Our awareness of how mass foodstuffs were now being produced was heightened and we questioned the how and the why of these changes. I suppose, aside from being part of the movement of the times, a major concern remained—how best to make food taste good. It had to be appealing to our palates.

It was 1971 and I was 21 years old when I encountered a taste experience I perceived as very different to that with which I had been brought up. The person who introduced me to this dish was to become a lifelong friend and one of my food mentors. The dish was Summer Pudding, and it was served at a New Year's celebration in Nelson where we were holidaying at my parents' place. I remember going home that evening and trying to describe the wonderful flavours and textures to my mother. It was an unusual and unexpected delight. Redcurrants, blackcurrants, raspberries, boysenberries (a Kiwi favourite) and strawberries were sealed in a casing made with stale white bread that had soaked up the tangy juice from the plentiful seasonal berries, staining the bread a magnificent rich purplish-red colour. Delicious.

My friend showed me how to make this simple dessert and it wasn't until years later, reading Elizabeth David's books, that I actually found a written recipe.

New Zealand summer pudding

Here is my Kiwi take on a favourite English dessert.

350g raspberries
200g boysenberries
55g redcurrants
55g blackcurrants
115g sugar
slices of one-day-old white bread, crusts removed

1 Put all the ingredients in a saucepan and simmer for 2 to 3 minutes or until the sugar has dissolved and the fruit is softening. Set aside to cool.
2 Line the base and sides of a round deep dish (I use a soufflé dish or a stainless steel bowl) with the bread. The dish needs to be completely lined. I cut the bread into triangles to achieve this and try to fit the pieces to the shape of the bowl.
3 Fill the lined bowl with the cooled mixed berries, taking care to strain off some of the excess juice (you can use this juice at the time of serving).
4 Cover the fruit with a layer of bread which again you have cut into shapes so as to snugly fit the top of the bowl. Cover with a dish that completely fits over the pudding. Put a 1.5kg weight on the plate and put the pudding in the fridge overnight. I have a piece of rock I keep for this purpose!
5 When ready to serve, turn the pudding out onto a dish. Serve with freshly whipped cream and the reserved juice.

SERVES 10–12

＊＊＊

Until then, I hadn't been interested in cooking; this was something my grandmothers and mother did. Yet, here was my friend Paula—someone my age—creating something to share that was so delicious I wanted to be able to make it. I was a poor student, married and the mother of a small child, but my curiosity had been aroused.

The tiny kitchen in our first small house followed by a succession of other smallish kitchens failed to hamper my cooking experiments. As my competence grew, the process of food preparation—the planning, the aromas, the warmth of it—calmed and contented me when intellectual pursuits and university study became too much. Cooking was my meditation, my way of coping when loneliness crept up or when confusion took over. Having someone to feed was always an essential part of the equation. It didn't seem right to make food and not have it enjoyed by others.

And so it was that we started hosting dinner parties. In the beginning, our guests had to bring their own chairs because we only had two. We did, however, have beautiful cutlery, crockery and glasses. We had married in style and there had been many such gifts to begin our life together. In those pre-hippy days our legs were long and boots were tight and high, our skirts were so short they were hardly decent, and real fur coats from our mothers' wardrobes were cut down to warm our upper bodies . . . after all, this was the Age of Aquarius.

With the cutlery and crockery, Elizabeth David's cookbooks had arrived as a wedding present along with the Siamese cat, Haytor Pianky, who lorded it over our small house, nibbling on delicacies from the kitchen. We may have been experimenting with most aspects of life at the time but Elizabeth David introduced us to French country cooking. So, a favourite dish of ours was a traditional French casserole, Boeuf Bourguignon. The delectable aromas of orange peel (my addition) and brandy, tiny onions, bacon bits, red wine, bay leaves and thyme filled our little cottage each Saturday afternoon in anticipation of an evening of sharing food and ideas, building lasting friendships, and talk of study, exams and dreams of the future.

Boeuf Bourguignon

1.5kg stewing steak (blade steak or gravy beef) cut into 3cm cubes
3–4 tbspn plain flour
2 tbspn olive oil
4 tbspn butter
250g bacon, cut into thick strips
3–4 medium shallots, finely chopped
2 cloves garlic, crushed to a paste with salt
375ml red wine (Burgundy or Pinot Noir)
375ml well-flavoured beef stock
1 tbspn tomato paste
1 bouquet garni (two sprigs each of parsley and thyme and 1 bay leaf tied together)
salt and freshly ground black pepper

18 small pickling onions, peeled
150g button mushrooms
finely chopped parsley to garnish

1 Preheat the oven to 170°C and lightly dust the meat with the flour.
2 Heat the oil and 1 tablespoon of butter in a heavy-based casserole dish.
3 Add the bacon and fry until crisp, then remove and set aside.
4 Add another tablespoon of butter and brown the meat in two or three batches, then add the shallots and garlic to the pan.
5 Fry for about 2 minutes, stirring constantly, then return all the meat to the dish.
6 Add the wine, stock, tomato paste, bouquet garni, salt and pepper and bring to a simmer.
7 Reduce the heat, cover the dish with the lid and place in the oven for about 1¾ hours.
8 Meanwhile, toss the onions in 1 tablespoon of butter in a frying pan until nicely brown.
9 Add to the casserole with the bacon, replace the lid and continue cooking for a further 20 minutes.
10 Brown the mushrooms in the last tablespoon of butter in the frying pan.
11 Add to the casserole and place in the oven for a further 10 minutes.
12 Take the casserole from the oven and transfer the meat and vegetables to a large hot serving platter.
13 Discard the bouquet garni.
14 Boil the liquid down so the sauce becomes concentrated and thickens a little.
15 Spoon the sauce over the meat and garnish with parsley.

SERVES 6

Later, more student days meant a shift to Dunedin. There was no money and no going out for the mother of a small baby living in a one-bedroom flat, with a husband who was a full-time student and social gadabout. There was no world travel or television, just long dark winter days, high ceilings and a beautiful new baby.

A pre-dinner game we played at the time was called 'Park Bench'. Baby asleep, we would put two chairs together in the middle of the room and one of us would sit there as if sitting alone in the park. Then the other would come along and sit down and see what happened. Would we converse? Would we notice each other? Where would it go? The outcome was always surprising.

One fine memory is of an eye fillet steak and a young husband desperate to impress. Not confident, he would try to make a dinner in the kitchen for his park-bench partner. I think there was eye fillet, new potatoes, salad and mushrooms. That sounded pretty easy, although the meat cost more than half the week's food budget. Dinner by candlelight. The steak was rare—much too rare—and afterwards there were dishes piled high in the kitchen. But it didn't matter, the people who'd met on the park bench were 'eating out' and enjoying the ambience of the flickering candlelight.

By the late 1970s vegetarianism had became the way of life for our young family along with the majority of our friends. It made sense—we wanted to be self-sufficient and we didn't like the idea of killing things. My fate was sealed when, armed with an axe as I had seen my grandmother be many times, I tried to kill one of the chickens. I caught the bird and laid it on a chopping block, taking aim down onto its neck. I don't remember much of the rest except 'running around like a headless chicken' took on new and negative meaning.

So, we didn't kill creatures, we ate dairy, vegetables and fruits and, even then, I was disturbed by the book *The Magic of Findhorns* set in Northern Scotland, which described the screaming of vegetables as they were pulled from the ground! The good thing to come from this acute sensitivity and awareness of the food we were preparing and ingesting was the development of a strong gratitude for what the earth could provide us, given the right circumstances, and the knowledge we were developing about ourselves as human beings and our physical needs.

The negatives were the obsessions regarding food, and the possibility of overdoing the 'healthy' bit as some of us became slaves to the ideals, to the rituals, so much so that we didn't have time to fully develop and explore other parts of our lives. We still remember the *Tassajara Cookbook* and the hours of bread preparation filling the house with warm, yeasty smells, the children helping with the kneading, and creating their own loaves. There were plaited loaves, rounded loaves, everyday loaves and special occasion loaves. One delicious yeasty offering remaining from that time is this large, sweet sticky bun, made by sister-in-law Robyn. It remains a family favourite.

Robyn's sticky bun

For a very special occasion, Robyn adds marzipan pieces to the cinnamon and raisin mixture and one red glacé cherry to each bun. This version is perfect for celebrations, particularly Christmas, with its red and white colour theme.

For the dough

1⅓ cups warm water
pinch of salt
2 tspsn sugar
2 tbspn melted butter or olive oil

4 tspn powdered yeast granules (I use Surebake)
3 cups plain white flour
1 egg, lightly beaten for egg wash
1 egg, lightly beaten for the dough

For the filling

zest and juice of one lemon
¼ cup soft brown sugar
1 cup large soft raisins
2 tspn powdered cinnamon
knob of butter

For the glaze

2 tbspn sugar
2 tbspn water

1 To make the dough, put the water, salt and sugar in a large bowl and sprinkle in the yeast. Set in a warm place to allow the yeast to 'work'.
2 When it looks fluffy, add the flour, 1 cup at a time, and the melted butter and 1 lightly beaten egg, stirring constantly.
3 Knead the mixture in the bowl until it becomes elastic. Cover the bowl and set in a warm place to rise until the dough has doubled in size.
4 Meanwhile, make the filling by putting the lemon juice, brown sugar, raisins and cinnamon in a small saucepan.
5 Gently warm the mixture until it melts together into a lovely velvety syrup, then add the lemon zest and butter. Set this mixture aside to cool.
6 Preheat the oven to 180°C. Grease a large baking tin—Robyn uses her largest roasting dish.
7 Tip the dough onto a floured board, punch down and knead for 10 minutes until nice and elastic again.
8 Roll out lightly to a long rectangular shape and spread the raisin mixture on the dough.

9   Roll the dough lengthways, as if you were making pinwheel scones. Pinch the edges together firmly.

10 Take a big sharp knife and cut through the sausage shape of rolled dough to make smaller 4cm-wide pieces.

11 Arrange the circular pieces as tightly together as possible in the centre of the tin in order to achieve a blossoming flower of fruit-filled bread. Remember the bread will spread as it cooks.

12 Brush the other beaten egg over the whole uncooked bun, cover and leave to rise again in a warm place for 10 to 15 minutes.

13 As soon as the bun starts to puff up, put it in the oven and bake for 25 minutes. You only want it to be golden on top. (Robyn tests her bun by opening the oven and tapping it; if it makes a slightly hollow sound she knows it's ready.)

14 When the bun is nearly ready to come out of the oven, make the glaze by putting the sugar and water in a heavy-based saucepan and heat, stirring all the time. As soon as the glaze starts to caramelise take it off the heat.

15 Remove the bun from the oven and arrange on a large serving platter. Brush the hot glaze over the whole bun.

SERVES 12–15, DEPENDING ON HOW GREEDY YOU ARE!

Those were the days of long hair, long dresses, Volkswagen Beetles and 'unkempt looking gatherings', as some people would have described them. We loved getting together in groups and we enjoyed sharing our living spaces, food offerings and, at times, our partners. They were the days of sharing.

Quiches and tarts had an important place in our household. The basic quiche consisted of a pastry shell made from home-ground or stone-ground flour and our favourite filling, usually spinach and cheese. Nowadays, we'd probably make it with bought filo pastry and call it spanakopita. Our 1970s version was rich and had a deep pastry base filled with eggs, cream, cheese and spinach, although, thinking about it now, it was probably made with silverbeet back then.

Spinach quiche

With baked potatoes and salad on the side, this is a filling and tasty meal for up to 10 people.

1 shortcrust pastry shell (see Perfect shortcrust pastry, page 46)

For the filling
1 large bunch fresh spinach or silverbeet leaves, washed and stalks removed
4 eggs
1½–2 cups cream and milk (half and half)
1 tbspn chopped chives (if available)
1 tbspn chopped parsley
salt and pepper, to taste
80–100g grated tasty cheese, or a half and half mix of parmesan and tasty
*   for a more delicate flavour*

1 Preheat the oven to 180°C.

2 Prepare the pastry shell, but don't blind bake.

3 Place the spinach or silverbeet in a large saucepan of boiling salted water and cook until wilted (just a few minutes). Drain and set aside.

4 Whisk the eggs and milk/cream together and season.

5 Place the cooled, cooked spinach onto the pastry and spread about evenly.

6 Sprinkle the herbs over the spinach.

7 Sprinkle the grated cheese on top.

8 Pour over the egg mixture and make a lattice pattern over the pie with any leftover pastry.

9 Bake for 30 to 45 minutes, or until the pastry looks cooked and the filling has puffed up.

SERVES 10

If you double the pastry recipe, the filling can be doubled to make a large and deep quiche.

I have a memory of the orange hessian curtains and small spaces of our second home, a brick labourer's cottage in Christchurch, with a kitchen so small two people found it difficult to be in it at the same time. Guests felt cramped in the tiny living room on many occasions, but the warmth of our friendships and the excitement of sharing ideas was uppermost. In that tiny room in front of the fireplace we explored how we were going to change the world.

Whenever there were problems, I cooked. The more difficult the problem, the more complicated the recipe required to calm the situation. Poached chicken on saffron rice was a recipe to overcome an extreme problem. Saffron was difficult to come by in New Zealand in the 1970s but, finally, all was ready. Our guest, who had some news to deliver, came in the back gate and walked up the path. I opened the door and greeted her, the kitchen emanating the warm, inviting aromas of poaching chicken and steaming saffron rice.

'I'm sorry, I forgot to mention I'm a vegan vegetarian,' she announced. My confidence seeping away, I welcomed her in, trying to think of an alternative meal to the one I had laboured over all afternoon. Here was me, trying to soften the way to our discussions and now we had a botched beginning to our new relationship. It was my first encounter with the word vegan. How did you feed a vegan?

I often used to make a baked cheesecake, with a biscuit and butter base and a luscious filling of Philadelphia cream cheese, eggs and sugar—it had a perfect texture when baked and we ate it with boysenberries and whipped cream. It's very rich and it's a bonus that it can be prepared a day before it is required.

Baked boysenberry cheesecake

This reliable offering from my kitchen was always popular. It's also delicious with cherries instead of boysenberries, for a change.

For the base
2 tbspn brown sugar
1½ cups crushed malt or arrowroot biscuits
1 tspn cinnamon
1 cup melted butter

For the filling

1 cup sugar
2 cups sour cream, softened
500g cream cheese
3 eggs
2 tspn vanilla
grated zest of an orange

For the topping

1 jar or can boysenberries

1 Preheat the oven to 170°C.
2 To make the base, mix all the ingredients together and press into the bottom of a deep 25cm springform tin.
3 To make the filling, beat all the ingredients together until smooth and pour into the crust.
4 Bake for 50 to 60 minutes, until the filling has set.
5 When cool remove from the tin, turn onto a serving platter and top with the boysenberries.
6 Serve with cream or yoghurt.

SERVES 12–14

CHAPTER 3

Idealism is in the air

Even when there was no money for material items or expensive outings, there was always a way found to provide a 'good table'. It was an echo of my grandmother's words, 'Hearth and home . . . make sure you remember the two,' she would say. So, even when the going got tough, food—its preparation and consumption—provided a framework and a rhythm to my days.

Coq au vin from Elizabeth David's *French Country Cooking* became a favourite, simmering slowly all afternoon in the ancient small oven in our lean-to kitchen, the mouthwatering aroma wafting through the cottage, and there was the added bonus that running the oven all afternoon helped warm the house.

Coq au vin

Of the many versions of coq au vin I've tasted and made over the years, I like the flavours of this one very much. You can easily adapt the recipe to make a smaller amount by using just one chicken and halving the other ingredients.

2 chickens (joint them into 8 pieces each or get the butcher to do it for you)
1 bottle red wine
3 bay leaves
some sprigs of thyme
salt and pepper
250g sliced bacon (I use streaky)
90g butter
20 or so baby onions
2 cloves crushed garlic
250g button mushrooms
40g plain white flour
1 tspn oil
½ cup brandy
4 cups chicken stock
2 tbsp tomato paste
1 extra tspn plain white flour
2 tspn chopped fresh parsley

1 Put the chicken pieces in a bowl and cover with the wine, bay leaves, thyme and a sprinkling of salt and pepper. Cover and refrigerate for 4 hours or overnight to marinate. At a pinch, if you are in a hurry 30 minutes will do.

2 Preheat the oven to 180°C.

3 Blanch the bacon in boiling water. Dry off and then chop. In a heavy-based casserole dish, sauté the bacon in 15g of the butter.

4 Add the onions and garlic and sauté until browned. Lift out and set aside.

5 Add another 15g of butter and cook the mushrooms.

6 Season with salt and pepper, then set aside with the onions and bacon.

7 Drain the chicken, keeping the marinade.

8 Pat the chicken pieces dry and coat in the flour.

9 Add the remaining butter and some oil to the casserole and fry the chicken pieces until golden brown. Remove the chicken from the casserole dish.

10 Add the brandy and deglaze the dish.

11 Place the chicken, the marinade, the chicken stock and the tomato paste, the mushrooms and bacon pieces into the casserole dish stirring gently to mix everything together and coat the chicken pieces. Put the lid on the casserole and cook in the oven for 1 to 1½ hours.

12 Before serving, taste and adjust the seasoning if required and discard the bay leaves. If sauce needs thickening, mix together the tbsp of flour with 1 tbsp water and whisk into the sauce. Reheat for a few minutes. Add the chopped parsley.

SERVES 8

During the late 1970s we began to have increasingly daring dinner parties. Like many experiences at the time, each event was something quite different, quite original and quite wonderful. On one occasion, the chef, a male friend, chose the venue—the second storey of an old stables, which was the site of his renovation project. Downstairs was a bomb site, an open courtyard where we used to all sit round a bonfire, among the dust and rubble. But this time he was having a dinner party, a formal one—the invitation had stated this. So dressed in our finery, second-hand or from our grandmothers' wardrobes, we duly attended. I wore a slinky, sexy red satin number, an old fox fur around my neck and elbow length gloves and had my hair in long golden ringlets. I don't remember my shoes, but no doubt they were high heels.

We arrived and were instructed to climb a ladder to the next level. There, a magnificent sight greeted us. A table running the full length of the stable loft was set for a banquet with an elaborate central table decoration of a luxuriant nature—there was a clay dragon, fruit, flowers and candles. There were a lot of us, maybe 25 plus, and I still remember the dessert, because it was the first time I had ever attended a dinner party with so many people and it was the first time I encountered this dessert. Layers of chocolate, crushed biscuit with butter and almonds cut into thin slices laid on the plate. It had been created by our host, who was well known for his inventiveness, not just with food, but with glass, wood and fast motorbikes.

Chocolate almond biscuit dessert

As no one kept the original recipe, I've adapted this from Rachel Grisewood's recipe for chocolate crunch.

550g dark chocolate
275g butter
4 tbspn golden syrup
400g milk arrowroot or malt biscuits, broken into chunks
1 cup slivered almonds, toasted

1 Grease a 30 × 20cm size tin and line it with baking paper.
2 Heat the chocolate, butter and golden syrup in a large saucepan over another saucepan of boiling water until the butter and chocolate are melted, stirring to combine.
3 Add the biscuit pieces and the slivered almonds and stir until they are well coated with the chocolate mixture.

4 Pour and then press mixture into the prepared tin. (It should be no more than 4cm deep.)

5 Cover with foil and refrigerate for at least 1 hour until set.

6 Cut into 16 small squares or 8 larger bar-shaped slices.

SERVES 8

All the men at the table that night were in formal attire. It was a white-tie occasion. Never mind if some of the suits were tails from another era. Never mind if not all the shirts were ironed or all the shoes black. In the candlelight they looked splendid, as did the women in their evening creations.

These were the days of my involvement with high fashion and modelling in Christchurch—when Tripe, the old butchery on Victoria Street, had been converted into a fashion boutique. Fashion parades were held there and we models changed into our gear in what had been the meat freezer. The lighting was murky and one night the wires to the lights festooned around the shop above the cat walk somehow became tangled with the ex-freezer door and gave one of the models a nasty shock. But the show went on, and it was fabulous, a prelude to even grander fashion events to come.

These people were working on the cusp of new things. We were a group of adventurers, not circumnavigating the globe but coming up with new ways of being in the world, which we perceived needed changing. There was flamboyance, an exoticness about the way we did things that, with a bit of dressing up, took us far from cold grey Christchurch nights. The dinner above the stables was one of those occasions. As the daring and experimentation escalated the adventuring began to take us in different directions, spilling out of town.

CHAPTER 4

Self-sufficiency and the daily grind

Some of our friends were ready to leave town and test themselves on the land. A group of them who were more serious about living out the self-sufficiency ideal settled in the small coastal township of Kaikoura. A variety of dwellings were developed on different properties, ranging from a cowshed adapted to living quarters on one property and railway carriages on another, to a large, drafty-but-roomy wooden two-storeyed house.

Daily life, however, was more communal. Social experiments were underway—it wasn't just about the food, although with well-tended gardens and lots of vegetables and fruit, I have memories of cook-ups (roasted mixed vegetables, beetroot salad, potato pies) for large numbers of people, including the extended families of the various households and their guests. I also remember hardship for the women preparing the food on wood stoves, and of a vague uneasy feeling that maybe things were going backwards, especially for women. Come on guys, it was the 1970s, perhaps there could be some concessions made to what technological progress had to offer?

Roast mixed vegetables

This is a modern take on our earlier baked vegetable dishes. If you're cooking for a crowd you may need to use two roasting dishes.

1kg mixed root vegetables (parsnips, kumara, baby carrots, beetroot, celeriac
*   and whole unpeeled garlic cloves)*
4 tbspn olive oil
2 tspn sweet smoked paprika
2 tspn cumin seeds
¼ cup honey
3 tbspn balsamic vinegar or sherry vinegar
1 tbspn finely chopped rosemary
sea salt
freshly ground black pepper

1 Preheat the oven to 180°C. Line a large roasting dish with baking paper.
2 Scrub the baby vegetables. Peel the larger vegetables and cut into large chunks.
3 Combine all the remaining ingredients in a large bowl. (If you don't have all the glazing ingredients, just oil, rosemary, salt and pepper will do.)
4 Add the vegetables, toss together to coat with the seasoning and place them in a single layer in the prepared dish.
5 Roast for about 40 minutes, turning the vegetables occasionally, until they are glazed and tender.

SERVES 6–8

Warm beetroot salad

The colours in this salad are wonderful.

10–12 small beets
2 red peppers, deseeded and cut into strips
2 red onions, finely sliced
2 tbspn olive oil
3 tbspn balsamic vinegar
3 tbspn honey
12-15 baby carrots
15–25 cherry tomatoes, cut in half
juice and zest of 1 lemon
fresh basil leaves, torn
salt and pepper, to taste

1 Prepare the beets by cutting off the leaves, leaving about 2cm of stalk at the top, and boiling them in water until tender. Remove the skins by rubbing gently with your fingers.
2 Toss the pepper and onion in the oil and put in a heavy-based frying pan. Cook until soft, then add the balsamic and honey and stir until caramelised.
3 Cook the carrots in boiling water until still firm to bite without being hard.
4 While the beets are still warm, place in a serving bowl.
5 Add the cooked peppers and onions, the carrots and lastly the tomatoes.
6 Top with the lemon juice and zest and sprinkle with basil leaves.
7 Season with salt and pepper and give everything a gentle stir.

SERVES 6-8

Potato cheese pie

This is rich and filling. Years later I learnt to make a dairy-free version by leaving out the cheese and using fresh chicken stock instead of milk. Red onions are also a good alternative for added sweetness.

4–5 large potatoes, peeled and sliced
2 large onions, sliced into rings
200–250g tasty cheese, grated or sliced
125ml milk
salt and pepper

1 Preheat the oven to 180°C.
2 Arrange the potatoes in a layer to cover the bottom of a 40cm baking dish.
3 Cover with a layer of onion rings, then a layer of cheese.
4 Repeat this until all the ingredients are used up, finishing with a layer of cheese.
5 Pour the milk in and season with salt and pepper.
6 Bake uncovered for 40 to 60 minutes until cooked through.

SERVES 4–6

The West Coast of the South Island, Nelson and Golden Bay, were areas where other friends and acquaintances pursued the ideal of self-sufficiency. Food preparation was labour intensive and mostly vegetarian. Looking back at diaries of the time I'm surprised and yet not surprised to see little or no mention made of these labours regarding food production and preparation. My diaries are full, but it's all about the angst of relationships, of love, connections, child rearing, the frustrations and dreams.

Always wanting more, impatient to feel more, do more, find the perfect relationship, always analysing people and their motives, trying to find a way through the maze. It was going to take us all a while to get there. And so we danced on, 'raging' at outdoor gatherings to the music of Jimi Hendrix, JJ Cale, Fleetwood Mac, The Rolling Stones, Van Morrison, Eric Clapton . . .

At these outdoor gatherings, high on the heat of the summer sun, with the music flowing through us, there was always the possibility of connection and love. We feasted on wholesome food and idealism.

I remember the baby born to a young couple in the two-storeyed house in Kaikoura. She had recently qualified as a doctor and he as a psychologist. The newborn baby's greeting to the world, which consisted of a dip in the freezing cold creek running through the back of the property, was a shock to me. This was part of a new way of doing things more closely connected to the natural world. Fortunately, the baby survived its rude welcome. These experiments were born of shared idealism. I felt like an onlooker—a city girl just passing through.

CHAPTER 5

Living in Australia

In 1979 Mark and I took our young family to Australia. We stopped in Sydney en route to our new home in Hobart, Tasmania. With the promise of a new decade, we were making a major change. I remember the excitement of crunching through filo pastry and biting into my first baklava. The dripping honeyed sweetness was superb—it was my first taste of Lebanese food, and I didn't have to make it myself. It was the beginning of a whole new trend—the time of regular eating out was upon us.

Prior to the 1980s in New Zealand, casual dining outside the home with children was rare. Now it was no longer just the fine dining experience for adults celebrating a special occasion—eating out was now possible for people of all ages and social milieux and the trend has continued to develop with more and more options. Then, the options began with pizza and pasta. As for wine, it was most often still bought in cardboard boxes filled with bladder-bagged red and white wine that we called 'Chateau Cardboard'.

Markets of all kinds were an exciting discovery for us in Australia. Fruit and vegetable markets, Saturday markets for breads, preserves, fruit and vegetables—all were new to me. Now, of course, farmers' and growers' markets are popular throughout New Zealand, but these were the first we had seen. We were also venturing into reintroducing red meat, chicken and fish to our diets.

Our friends and social setting in Tasmania in the early 1980s included people from widely differing socio-economic backgrounds and ideologies. We still encountered and enjoyed the 'living off the land' vegetarian idealists, but we were also mixing with a more sophisticated group of professional friends who ate European-style food. The passing on of ideas continued, new influences to modify our earlier habits and new foods adding variety to our diets.

The move to Tasmania also provided an escape from things and relationships at home that had gone wrong in the pursuit of self-awareness. A clown workshop, a new baby, a new friend and an upside-down lemon meringue pie with no pie crust pretty well summed things up. That pie provided my first connection with Tasmania at that time. The tangy lemon tastes fresh and pure, the softness of the meringue—there are no sharp edges and the absence of pastry, which can be so varied depending on the skills of the chef, is a relief.

Upside-down crustless lemon meringue pie

It's no wonder Eli's light and delicious dessert remains a firm family favourite.

4 eggs, separated
1 cup sugar
45g butter

grated rind of 1 lemon
juice of 1½ lemons
300ml cream

1 Preheat the oven to 180°C. Grease a flan or pie dish.
2 Beat the egg whites until stiff.
3 Add half of the sugar slowly and continue beating until the whites are holding their shape, forming soft peaks when you lift out the beater.
4 Put the meringue mix into the dish and bake for 15 to 20 minutes.
5 Take the meringue out of the oven and set aside to cool.
6 Heat the egg yolks, remaining sugar, butter, rind and lemon juice in a separate ceramic bowl over a saucepan of boiling water, stirring for 15 to 20 minutes until thick and creamy. Top the meringue with the filling.
7 When the filling is completely cool, decorate with whipped cream.

SERVES 6

Our first Christmas in Tasmania was as I remembered Christmas from my childhood. I was comforted by the invitation for our family to join Diana, the local theatre director I had begun to work for, and her husband, John, to share their very traditional English Christmas celebration. Silver service, roast turkey, Christmas pudding with brandy butter and threepences. When I was young we also used to find threepences in our Christmas pudding—they were the smallest silver coin in the currency at the time. The change to decimal currency changed all of that for us and nowadays, of course, there is no equivalent.

Christmas pudding

Over the years I have adapted various recipes and this is the result, which we now all enjoy each year. It makes a medium-sized pudding, which provides about 15 servings. If you wish, add boiled silver coins into the pudding mixture before it goes into the pudding basin. Note that you should only use silver coins, which must be sterilised before use. Alternatively, you could wrap your coins tightly in tinfoil.

175g butter
150g brown sugar
3 eggs
1 cup plain flour
1 cup fresh breadcrumbs
15g raisins
175g currants
1 grated apple
½ cup candied orange peel
½ tbspn freshly grated nutmeg
1 tspn salt
¼ tspn ground mace
½ cup brandy

1 Grease a 1.5l pudding basin. (If you don't have one a bowl will do.)
2 Cream the butter and sugar.
3 Add the eggs and beat until well combined.
4 Add the remaining ingredients and mix to combine.
5 Pour the mixture into the prepared basin and cover with baking paper. Secure lightly around the rim.
6 Simmer over a saucepan of water for about 5 hours—remember to keep refilling the pot with water. I usually partially cook my pudding two or

three days before Christmas Day and store it in the fridge until ready to complete the cooking on Christmas Day, when it needs to be boiled for 2 to 3 hours. The trick is to cook it just long enough so that the centre is cooked without drying out the rest of the pudding.

7 To serve, tip the pudding onto a serving dish and take it to the table.

8 Pour over the brandy and immediately set it alight—it will burn quite briefly, but spectacularly. It is fun to watch but on a bright sunny New Zealand-summer Christmas Day it doesn't have quite the same effect as it does on a dark wintry day in Europe.

SERVES 15

And you can't have Christmas pudding without brandy butter!

Brandy butter

This is delicious with warm Christmas pudding or fruit mince pies. Stored in the fridge, it keeps for ages.

150g icing sugar
100g butter, softened
20ml brandy

1 Mix all the ingredients together until well blended and store in the fridge until ready to use.

2 Use sparingly.

Later, our baby boy's Name-Day ceremony was held at 'Ashfield', the home of our new friends, Roger and Barbara. He was the solicitor general and Barb was his wife extraordinaire. With a huge and glorious garden, a beautiful house, and a taste for and an ability to prepare delicious meals, Barb became a food mentor for me. To celebrate our new baby we had a most delicious rich chocolate cake.

Name-Day chocolate cake

You can serve this cake as a dessert with a syrup of orange juice, sugar and zest poured over the cake slices or you can make a ganache, ice the cake and serve it with tea.

220g caster sugar
100g dark chocolate (64% cocoa solids), finely chopped
¼ cup hot water
2 egg yolks
40g plain flour
60g cocoa (Dutch process, if you can)
4 egg whites

1 Preheat the oven to 160°C. Lightly grease a 20cm springform tin.
2 Heat 165g of the sugar, the chocolate and hot water in a bowl over a saucepan of simmering water and stir until smooth.
3 Remove from the heat, then add the egg yolks and mix to combine.
4 Fold in the flour and then the cocoa.
5 In a separate bowl, whisk or beat the egg whites until soft peaks form. Add the remaining sugar and whisk to combine.
6 Carefully fold the egg whites into the chocolate mixture.

7 Pour the mixture into the prepared tin and bake for 30 to 40 minutes until risen and firm to touch. Test with a skewer and remove the cake from the oven when the centre is still slightly soft.

8 Turn the cake out of the tin onto a wire rack to cool.

SERVES 8

My friendship with Barb continued to develop over the next three decades, long after we left Tasmania, but we had many happy days, family days, during our time there. There was the famous Salamanca Market in Hobart every weekend and, for me, theatre work again. When we returned to New Zealand I had changed and arrived home with new enthusiasm for both my home-making and my theatre career.

CHAPTER 6

The return home

The year was 1981. In our two-year absence, outdoor markets and outdoor café eating had arrived in New Zealand. There was a proliferation of eating establishments. Although busy making careers and growing a business and keeping our family tended, we were still trying to live the 'good life'. There were ponies to feed and goats to tend.

I dreamed of starting up a goat farm. Freesia, our nanny goat, gave birth to triplet bucks that first year—not much profit in that. Ponies came and went. One, called Patch, gave birth to a most glorious replica of herself, a tiny skewbald with spots in all the right places. The children were overwhelmed with delight. The foal was so small you could lift him in your arms.

The house and property were filled to overflowing with children and pets, cat and kittens, lambs, one for each year, goats times three on long tethers in the front paddock, ponies times three, chickens and even a cockatoo. The neighbours felt uncomfortable—the hippies are back next door! Maybe, I didn't want that label anymore. After all, I had experienced sophistication in Hobart—I knew how it was done and I wanted to try at home.

I decided to put on a ladies' lunch. My guest was particularly elegant—someone making her way in the world of fashion at the time. I planned to serve a courgette quiche (with home-made pastry, of course) with a salad and a lemon loaf cake to follow. When the day for the lunch arrived, the house was tidy and still, the sun was out. I was well prepared. We sat down to a nicely set table—it was a black lacquered oak table retrieved from the family bach, where it had been used for table tennis for many years.

My confidence was high. I knew I could do it again—I could entertain at home. There had been a bit of a gap—a few years getting family and our careers into some sort of shape—but now, here I was I thought, beginning to entertain, once again, in style.

Perfect shortcrust pastry

This is the recipe for pastry I've used with success over many years. So easy and quick to make, it suits a variety of dishes requiring pastry. You can also freeze the pastry until required—it's very handy to have a ball of pastry ready and waiting in the freezer.

150g plain flour
½ tspn salt
pinch of sugar
115g chilled butter, cut into 1cm cubes
4–4½ tbspn cold water

1 Place the flour, salt, sugar and butter in a food processor (I use a Magimix) and blend until the mixture is crumbly. Add the water and continue processing. Within a few minutes the mixture will have formed into a rough ball. Take it out of the processor, roll into a smooth ball, cover it with plastic wrap and place in the fridge for a minimum of

2 hours (or overnight). When ready to use, roll the pastry out as quickly as possible so it doesn't soften and become difficult to handle.

2 Sprinkle the board and top of the pastry with flour as necessary to stop sticking. Lift and turn the dough as it grows with rolling.

3 The dough should be used as soon as it is rolled out.

Courgette quiche

1 batch Perfect shortcrust pastry (see opposite)

For the filling
3–4 small freshly picked courgettes
3 eggs
1 cup cream
1 cup milk
salt and pepper
80g strong cheese (tasty cheddar or parmesan), grated

1 Preheat the oven to 180°C.

2 Prepare the shell by rolling the pastry into a circle about ¼cm thick and about 5cm larger than a springform tin or loose-bottom flan tin and line the base and sides of the dish.

3 Line the pastry shell with baking paper and weight the paper down with dried beans. Bake for 8 to 10 minutes.

4 Remove the paper and the beans, prick the bottom of the pastry and then put back in the oven for another 2 or 3 minutes or until the shell is beginning to turn a lovely golden-brown colour.

5 Turn the oven down to 160°C.

6 Grate the courgettes and place in the cooked shell.

7 In a bowl, whisk the eggs, cream, milk and salt and pepper, then pour the mixture over the courgettes and top with the cheese.

8 Bake for 20 minutes or until the filling is puffed up.

SERVES 6

✳✳✳

My guest and I chatted as we ate our lunch. The quiche went down well, and then the salad. She leant forward to serve herself . . . and that's when I heard our cockatoo, Baraud, wings batting furiously as he tried to balance himself. I'd forgotten to put him away in his cage and now here he was, making a low pass over our table. B made one further pass across the table, revealing very unkempt tail feathers, then settled with a screech up in the ceiling rafters. My poor guest was startled. I apologised profusely as I hastily removed the now tainted salad that B's tail feathers had contacted on his low fly-over.

My guest and I tried to recover and we began discussing the latest trend of coloured pantyhose when, through the French doors, came Lamb Lamb, the number-one pet lamb, now a few months old. Still thinking he was our baby, this overjoyed woolly creature trotted straight into the dining room. Cursing myself for not securing him properly, I removed him from the house and, as I did so, I reflected on the commonsense of our neighbour's recent threat when Lamb Lamb had visited his property uninvited. 'Good fences make good neighbours,' boomed Bill across our makeshift fence, 'and yours doesn't make the grade. Build a decent fence, keep your livestock off my property or your lamb will be Sunday lunch.'

Crossing and uncrossing her long slender legs, my guest was looking dismally uncomfortable. And that's when the finale of our wild and woolly pet parade put paid to any future dining opportunities with my elegant guest. We lived near a stream and the area at that time was quite rural. Wild creatures, much loved as characters in literature such as Ratty and Mole from *The Wind in the Willows*, were only seen as a threat when they invaded our domestic habitat. Our lunch came to an abrupt end when a large bedraggled water rat wandered past on the wall outside the dining room. And we hadn't even got to dessert.

This was the era of pot-luck meals. Rules were devised to protect the host from a disastrous display. A rough menu would be worked out in advance and people asked to bring a dish from this framework. Could you bring a salad? a green salad? a vegetable salad? a rice salad? Could you bring a main dish? something vegetarian? chicken? beef? Could you bring an entrée? There was the occasional severe blip when a guest asked to bring pre-dinner nibbles turned up after dessert, but mostly the system worked pretty well and some wonderful feasting ensued.

Rice salad

This salad is a great contribution to a pot-luck meal.

For the salad
3 cups cooked long grain rice
100g chopped walnuts
1 stalk chopped celery
1 grated carrot
fresh herbs, chopped (mint, marjoram, parsley)
salt and pepper
1 spring onion, finely chopped

For the dressing

2 tbspn vinegar
1 clove crushed garlic
2 tbspn olive oil
2 tspn lemon juice
2 tspn soy sauce

1 Put all the salad ingredients in a serving bowl.
2 To make the dressing, put all the ingredients into a shaker or screw-top jar and shake to combine. Pour over the rice and stir the dressing through the salad.

SERVES 6

Another simple but tasty salad of the time was made with grated carrots, a handful of currants or chopped raisins, the zest and juice of an orange and a teaspoon of sugar, all mixed together. It is something children find easy to make and they always enjoy the naturally sweet flavour.

CHAPTER 7

First taste of Europe

During the 1980s I became the lucky recipient of my sister Angie's airline discount. My life began to change rapidly as my food experiences expanded beyond Australasia. I began to see and taste the food I'd been reading about and looking at in recipe books and travel magazines for years. There was no turning back. In France I was fully captured by clean fresh flavours, uncluttered plates, perfect produce of the season, delicious sauces, traditional foods being maintained where appropriate, long lunches, a variety of wines and adventures with fungi.

Back home, we modified our diets as our tastes refined. With more imported foods on our grocery shelves and more dollars in our pockets to buy imported foodstuffs, a whole new era of food preparation and presentation began. It's hard to believe how short that history is when we look at what we can now enjoy at home and how New Zealand is celebrated internationally as a food producer.

We all have stories of travel and food. In my mind, one of the reasons for travel is to taste and experience new food in all its forms. We have an incorrigible appetite for the new, even if we later become sophisticated and dismissive.

In 1988, the main warning to travellers was 'Don't carry large quantities of cash in your pocket or wallet, or your wallet in a hip pocket. Don't carry more cheques than you need. Remember tourists are targets.' It made it all sound much more difficult and dangerous than it really was.

After a brief visit to the UK, enjoying the hospitality of my 'summer pudding' friend from twenty years before, it was on to France. This was the first of many visits to France, staying with family in the Dordogne region. Twelve hundred hectares of farmland and forest. The memory of the extraordinary beauty of this countryside remains with me, along with the wonderful indulgence of rising from my *chambre* in the morning and opening first the windows, then the heavy wooden shutters, and looking out onto pastures and the quiet forest beyond.

The food was everything I had fantasised about. The family's cook came that first day and made a ratatouille—'Yum', was my diary comment that night. Ratatouille became deeply imbedded in my taste memory that day so that every time I cook it now it evokes memories and feelings associated with that first French experience. The rich flavours of long, slow cooking, the warm aromas of thyme and bay leaves escaping from under the casserole lid and the strong colours of red pepper, purple aubergine and green courgette, all freshly picked from the late-summer vegetable patch—a food memory I cherish.

Ratatouille—the French way

This recipe makes a large quantity of ratatouille when you have an over abundance of the ingredients in your summer garden. Ratatouille can be bottled or frozen—I once made some, packed the jars in a box and couriered them to Auckland to my son, who had just moved there. Now I can't believe I did this and I wonder if he ever ate them?

1kg aubergines, diced
salt
olive oil, for frying
1kg mixed green and yellow courgettes, diced
1kg onions, skinned and sliced
3 green peppers, deseeded and sliced
2 red peppers, deseeded and sliced
2 chillies, deseeded and sliced (optional)
5kg tomatoes, skinned and crushed
2-3 garlic cloves, skinned and crushed
fresh herbs, such as thyme, bay leaves, basil, oregano, parsley, to taste
salt and pepper, to taste

1 Place the diced aubergines in a colander and sprinkle liberally with salt. The original French recipe says to leave for an hour but I only leave for 5 to 10 minutes and it still seems to get rid of excess juices. Rinse and pat dry with absorbent paper towels. If you're in a huge hurry, leave this step out altogether—there won't be any dire consequences!

2 Heat the oil in a frying pan and gently fry the aubergine and then transfer it to a large saucepan or casserole dish. Continue frying the courgettes, onions, peppers and chillies separately, transferring all to the saucepan or casserole. Add the chopped tomatoes, garlic, herbs (except for bay leaves, if using) and season. Cover and simmer for 1 to 2 hours either on the element or in the oven.

3 Preheat the oven to 90°C.

4 Place the ratatouille in sterilised preserving jars, drizzle with a little olive oil and add one bay leaf to each jar. Seal the jars by placing in the oven for 30 minutes.

5 This is also suitable for freezing in plastic containers.

MAKES 4–5 LITRES

On the second day, I was introduced to food shopping, French-village style, as we bought the ingredients for an outdoor lunch—local paté, saucisson, tomatoes for a simple salade tomate, bread, cheese, grapes and sweet treats were purchased. Straightaway, I began to learn about simplicity and perfection, of years of skill being passed down, resulting in the perfect paté. Already, I am in love with this place and its food.

Over the following days we dine on Madame E's casserole and turnips and Madame A's wild chevreuil (roe deer). All are accompanied by wines of the region that are so inexpensive but so good. Amidst all the wonderful food I struggle with the language and with 'finding my place'. Happily, my awkwardness continues to be overcome by superb food experiences.

There is a visit to an ancient flour mill beside a stream, with a water wheel that still runs the mill, and there's a boulangerie and pâtisserie attached. I remember the heavenly smells of bread baking in the wood-fired oven, and the nearby press where fresh walnuts are having their oil extracted.

There is another memorable meal back with family at the petit château—canard (duck) for the main and tarte aux mures (blackberry tart) and fromage frais for dessert. It was blackberry season and the berries were fat and juicy—a taste of the forest brought to the table.

Sweet short pastry

This is a good recipe that I have used for years.

110–115g plain flour
55g sugar
55g butter
1 egg yolk
3 tbspn water

1 Place the flour, sugar and butter in a food processor (I use a Magimix) and blend until the mixture is crumbly. Add the egg yolk and water and continue processing. Within a few minutes the dough will have formed into a rough ball. Take it out of the processor, roll into a smooth ball, wrap in plastic wrap and place in the refrigerator for a minimum of 2 hours (or overnight).

Tarte aux mures

My nieces in the kitchen at the family chateau in the Dordogne showed me how to roll the fat berries in sugar to thickly coat them before placing them in the tart shell for baking.

1 batch Sweet short pastry (see above)

For the filling
1 cup sugar
3–4 cups freshly picked blackberries

1 Roll the pastry out as quickly as possible so it doesn't soften and become difficult to handle.
2 Sprinkle the board and top of the pastry with flour, as required, to stop sticking. Lift and turn the dough as it grows with rolling.
3 Roll into a circle about ¼cm thick and about 5cm larger all around than the tin or flan ring you are using. Line the base and sides.
4 Preheat the oven to 220°C.
5 Sprinkle a thin coating of white sugar onto the pastry base.
6 Sprinkle the remaining sugar over the blackberries and toss until the berries are coated. Place the sugary fruit into the pastry shell.
7 Bake for 10 minutes then turn the oven down to between 150°C and 160°C and bake for a further 20 minutes or until the pastry is cooked.
8 Serve immediately with dollops of whipped cream. Delicious.

SERVES 4–6

Over the years and visits to different regions, I learnt many small cooking tricks from the French, including the short cut to skinning red peppers when making poivron aux olives, or to use cold in any dish. Simply bake the red peppers whole in a hot oven until the skins go black, and then get them out of the oven somehow (this is the hard bit) without burning your hands or having them collapse in a sloppy heap before you can manoeuvre them over to the waiting plastic bag. Seal the plastic bag and they will sweat, loosening their skins, the stem and their seeds. When cool, take out and discard the skins, seeds and stems.

On the other hand, I saw some tricks which definitely did not impress or amuse me. One evening in a small, isolated routier (roadside café) on a long, flat stretch of road with crop stubble burning on both sides of the road, we sat at a table next to a group of truck drivers. They were enjoying each other's company and the food. One of them had a box that he proudly opened at the table. It was full of baby turtles destined for some diner's delight, but in the meantime they were the truckies' playthings. The men poured their wine into bowls, putting the turtles into the wine and then onto the table to watch their drunken antics. It was horrible.

Associated with this memory is the plate of thin slices of something vaguely resembling salami that I had ordered, but the taste, texture and visuals were all wrong. It turned out to be cow's cheek, set in aspic and then sliced. I was alerted to the fact that I must take more care with my ordering. Interestingly, this cut of meat (a tough and lean cut) is making a come back in restaurants in New Zealand and Australia. Braising and slow cooking give the best result.

I realised early in Paris that here was a part of France where wonderful French food was hard to come by for the uninitiated tourist. So many of Paris's eating establishments were designed to capture visitors and were not great examples of French cooking. Unless you have some inside knowledge about where to go or a large wallet and are staying at one of the more prestigious addresses, you can be disappointed by Parisian cuisine.

In the 1980s what we found was very much hit and miss as a couple of my diary extracts from 1988 testify: 'Not nice meal—horrible beef bourguignon', in one establishment to expressions of excitement over a crème caramel in another. Here's my recipe for crème caramel that has been developed and improved over many years.

Crème caramel

This reliable delicious crème caramel can be made the day before you need it. It's also the most perfect dish for anyone with sensitive digestion as it soothes and energises.

To make it with any degree of success, it's essential you have a heavy-based reducing pan for the caramel, 8 individual ceramic ramekins and a large heavy dish to use as the water bath to sit the ramekins in for cooking.

For the caramel
110–115g granulated sugar
40ml cold water

For the custard
600ml milk
1 vanilla bean
3 eggs
3 extra egg yolks (you can save the whites for Pavlova, see page 1) or a
*   batch of meringues (page 121)*
85g granulated sugar

1   Preheat the oven to 160°C.
2   To make the caramel, heat the sugar and water in a heavy-based pan over moderate heat, swirling frequently, until the syrup caramelises. Watch the mixture carefully as it burns easily. Sometimes I have had to make this up to three times to get it just right; the trick is not to walk away!
3   Place 8 ramekins into a heavy baking dish and pour hot water into the dish until it comes about halfway up the sides of the ramekins.
4   When the caramel mixture is ready, very quickly pour a little into the bottom of each ramekin. It will set straightaway.

5 To make the custard, heat the milk and vanilla bean over a medium heat and allow to simmer briefly. Set aside to cool and remove the vanilla bean.

6 Beat the eggs, yolks and sugar together and add this mixture to the milk. Beat until foamy. While still warm, strain the mixture into a pouring jug and pour an equal amount into each ramekin.

7 Bake for about 40 minutes or until set—you can test with a skewer, which should come out clean.

8 Take the ramekins from the water bath and place on a wire rack to cool. Chill in the fridge until ready to serve.

9 To serve, turn out onto serving dishes.

SERVES 8

Like many other newcomers to Paris with language difficulties and feeling desperately hungry, we ended up in the Quartier Latin. There, food merchants beckon from every direction. Sadly, most of them are not French. It wasn't until much later—in the late 1990s and early 2000s—that the gastronomy of Paris began to reveal itself to me.

After first discovering the joys of France, we ventured into Italy. By then, it was late summer—hot and muggy—and the air was thick and heavy, the heat radiating from the walls and the walkways, accentuating the hazy orange glow from the roof tiles of Florence. We had to find a place to have a picnic. It needed to be leafy, green and cool, and it needed to be away from people. First we had the delightful experience of assembling the food. Here's my diary entry for this pleasurable exercise that awakened all our senses:

A picnic in Florence. First the collection of the goodies. We had baskets newly purchased in France, minimal Italian, a few thousand lire and a lot of enthusiasm. Excited by the amount of colour in the food displays, it was very tempting to lean over and hover and try to choose which piece of fruit. We were quickly stopped in our tracks by an attendant who appeared from nowhere indicating we were to look, not touch. She would pick the fruit up. We collected a picnic of delicacies of the area, each wonderful food item so beautifully wrapped in tissue paper, then brown paper, then bagged. Often the bags were decorated with images particular to the shop. In the final picnic there was an eggplant dish, an artichoke dish, cheeses, salamis, 'pane' bread (weighed and priced by the kilo) and finally some little seasonal berries.

The men would lead the way and find us the ideal spot. As our stomachs were sending hungry messages we tramped on up and beyond the city centre. There ahead was a huge imposing gate and, beyond, a building, also very imposing, but beyond that, rolling lawns and trees, a park, perfect for a picnic and no people in sight. That was strange, we thought, but no matter, we would just go in. We quickly and quietly walked through the front gates and wandered across the beautifully kept grass until we reached a group of trees. We spread our picnic out and had time to take a few photos and each savour a few morsels when, suddenly, our peace was broken by the arrival of numbers of police or security guards, all carrying weapons and shouting loudly and pointing to the large building, then the gates—it appeared we had let ourselves into some sort of government establishment where picnicking was most certainly not allowed. We collected up our uneaten food and quickly headed out through the gates and into the city.

That first visit to Italy is remembered for many faux pas—like picnicking in the wrong place—but, also, for many delicious new food experiences. The list is long: insalata di mare (seafood salad with small octopuses), ravioli de casa (pasta parcels with ricotta and spinach filling), biscotti (crunchy twice-baked biscuits that are a perfect match with the ubiquitous espresso) and, most delicious of all, gelato (ice cream made with full-cream milk, egg yolks and sugar). We thought we were in heaven!

Ravioli de casa

This recipe comes courtesy of David Rumens, head chef at Freemans in Lyttelton, Christchurch. We have been lucky enough to enjoy his Italian cuisine and the friendly service of Freeman's staff for many years, making its re-emergence following the February 2011 earthquake (which closed the restaurant for 10 months) an especially welcome event.

The combination of the rich, creamy filling in delicate pasta parcels and the buttery sauce will transport your tastebuds to Italy.

For the filling
4 large aubergines
olive oil
1½ cups grated parmesan
1 garlic bulb, roasted and squeezed to release the paste-like cloves or ½ tspn
    finely chopped garlic
salt and ground black pepper
150g taleggio (a soft Italian cow's milk cheese)

For the pasta
220 g plain flour
salt
2 eggs

For the buttery pasta sauce
500g cherry tomatoes, halved
a few fresh basil leaves, torn into pieces
a little water from cooking the pasta
6 tbspn butter
freshly grated parmesan, to serve

1. Preheat the oven to 180°C.
2. To make the filling, split the aubergines in half lengthways and score them on the cut side with a sharp knife.
3. Place in an oven pan skin-side down, with olive oil, and sprinkle with salt. Roast until they are soft.
4. Once cooked, scoop out the flesh, roughly chop it and add the grated parmesan and garlic. (You can roast the aubergines the day before if you like. If you do this, leave the scooped-out flesh to drain in a colander overnight with a bowl under the colander to catch the liquid. This makes for a drier filling.)
5. Season with salt and ground pepper.
6. To make the pasta, sift the flour and a pinch of salt into a mound on a work surface.
7. Make a well in the centre and break the eggs into it. Work the mixture until a soft dough forms.
8. Form the dough into a ball and wrap in plastic wrap until ready to use. You need to leave at least half an hour.
9. Roll out the dough as thinly as possible. (This is best done with a pasta machine, but if you're feeling energetic it can be done with a rolling pin.)
10. Cut the dough into circles approximately 5cm in diameter.

11 Place about 1 teaspoon of the filling mixture on each dough circle.

12 Dice the taleggio into 1cm cubes and place one piece on the top of each mound of filling before folding over the ravioli. To seal you can use either an egg wash or water. Wet the edge of the pasta circle, fold it in half over the filling and firmly pinch the edges to seal in the filling.

13 To serve, bring a large saucepan of water to the boil and add a little salt and a splash of oil to the water. Cook the ravioli in the salted water for approximately 4 to 6 minutes (depending on the thickness) until al dente, then drain.

14 While the pasta is cooking, make the sauce by placing all the ingredients except the parmesan in a saucepan to melt and mix together, shaking the pan to distribute the ingredients.

15 Divide the pasta into 6 pasta bowls or place in a large serving dish. Pour the sauce over the pasta and toss gently to coat with the sauce. Serve with a dish of freshly grated parmesan on the side.

SERVES 6

Gelato al limone

Blackberry granita (see page 76) makes a wonderful accompaniment to this as a refreshing summer dessert.

1 cup milk
1 cup sugar
5 egg yolks
3 tbs coarsely grated lemon peel
2 cups cream
¾ cup lemon juice

1　Heat milk over low heat, stir in sugar.

2　Add lemon peel and keep on low heat.

3　Whisk egg yolks and add to milk mixture. Cook and stir over low heat until mixture thickens.

4　Remove from heat and stir in lemon juice. Strain and allow to cool.

5　Lightly whip cream.

6　Fold the cream into the lemon custard mixture.

7　Put in a container, cover and freeze. Take out and stir at intervals. It will be ready in about 3 hours.

MAKES 1 LITRE (SERVES 4-6).

San Gimignano was another highlight of that first trip to Italy. A UNESCO World Heritage Site, it is two hours by bus from Florence. I'll never forget the day we had lunch stretched out on the dry grass under some olive trees at the top of the hill above the tiny fortified town—Tuscan sausages (those wonderful, tasty, dry sausages that hang from the rafters in food stores ready for the buyer to inspect) served simply with a hunk of rustic bread, local cheeses and fruit that tastes of sunshine left an indelible impression on me.

On our first trip to Europe we also visited Stockholm. When we arrived the sky was a glorious blue and we enjoyed the golden weather of late autumn. The Dalai Lama was in town and we were lucky enough to see him as he arrived to address a large gathering of people at Stockholm Cathedral in the old town. Anti-apartheid protesters were marching, and the experience was altogether quite unexpected.

By chance, we had booked into a lovely bed and breakfast run by Mrs Eva Gesslar, in her beautiful home in central Stockholm. It was a traditional Swedish house, with parquet floors, Turkish rugs and ancient traditional wooden furniture. The walls were graced by original watercolours depicting Swedish flora and fauna. Our room was a place of tranquility and beauty. On the desk was a porcelain version of Medusa with the head hollowed and in it was a creeping plant, its tendrils curving down Medusa's face to form her hair.

The breakfast tray on our first morning in Stockholm, so thoughtfully prepared by Mrs Gesslar, is the thing I remember most. It was set with silver cutlery and there was a silver dish covering the butter, three different types of bread, including a type of pumpernickel, and toast with thin slices of cheese and butter that had been rounded and smoothed to a perfect shape, sitting in a small glass dish. There was a choice of tea and strong coffee, both in silver pots. This simple breakfast, perfectly presented, made a lasting impression.

Later that day, when we got off the train in Uppsala enroute to Österbybruk, about 200 kilometres north of Stockholm, we learned more about local cuisine. There, our host cooked a traditional Swedish dinner of meat patties with a sauce made from fungi that we had gathered in the forest that afternoon and lingonberry sauce accompanied by potatoes and green salad. We also helped pick the lingonberries, which are small, round and dark red when ripe. They grow wild, close to the ground and take a lot of patience to harvest, but they are full of flavour and goodness so it is worth the effort. Dessert was a sugar cake served with ice cream and cloudberry sauce.

This was all washed down with imported wine (it was purchased from various European wine merchants and then mixed in Sweden for local consumption). There were stringent laws about alcohol in Sweden – it could only be purchased in government-monitored stores. I noted at the time that the traffic accident rate was extremely low. Other information we gathered over dinner time conversations during our visit included hearing it was against the law for teachers and parents to apply corporal punishment to children, and that every schoolchild in Sweden was provided with a hot meal at lunchtime, free of charge.

At the Unga Klara Theatre, in Stockholm, I saw a rehearsal of *In the Summer House* (*I Lusthuset*) by Jane Bowles. It was directed by Suzanne Osten. Suzanne is famous in Sweden and beyond for her production and direction of provocative theatre for young people. The play was two and a half hours long and I couldn't understand the Swedish, but I have never forgotten the profound effect it had on me. The stage covered with water, ladders to the ceilings, angst-ridden mothers and tearaway young daughters scaling the ladders captivated the teen audience. I took these ideas about risk-taking in theatre production back with me to my work with youth theatre in New Zealand. I also returned with a determination to create beauty and quality in my food preparation. The ingredients might be different in many parts of the world, but the idea of celebration, even of the simplest breakfast, would not be forgotten.

Swedish meat patties

In Sweden they sometimes use wild game meat finely minced, but here we can use high-quality beef mince. We ate these in Sweden with lingonberry sauce. The sauce recipe below can be adapted to use fresh or frozen cranberries. Alternatively, I like to serve the patties with porcini sauce, from Katie's recipe (see page 196) with the caraway seeds.

600g minced beef
4 egg yolks
1 onion finely diced
1 anchovy fillet
2 tbsp capers
1 tbsp mustard (I use Dijon)
1 large potato, cooked and diced
Salt
100g butter
pepper

1 Place mince, egg yolks, finely diced onion, salt and pepper into a bowl and mix well.
2 Add chopped capers, anchovy and diced potato. Mix all ingredients well.
3 Shape into 4 to 6 large patties or 8 medium.
4 Fry patties in a heavy based pan with butter until browned on both sides. You will need to do this in batches.
5 Place the patties in a baking dish and cover with tinfoil and cook in an oven at 160°C for a further 15 minutes. To retain the moisture you could put some of the fungi sauce you are using around the patties in the baking dish.
6 Serve patties with cubed fried potatoes with fungi sauce of your choice and with lingonberry or cranberry sauce on the side.

Lingonberry Sauce

4 cups lingonberries
½ cup water
1 cup sugar

1 Prepare berries by picking out stalks and leaves.
2 Place in saucepan. Add water and heat to boiling.
3 Add sugar and simmer 10 minutes.
4 Remove from heat and place saucepan in cold water. Stir the fruit mixture for 1-2 minutes.

SERVE COLD. MAKES 3 CUPS.

Swedish sugar cake

This is a rather plain cake that works well with fruit and cream. Use a bundt tin, (they have a hole in the middle).

50g butter
200g sugar
190g flour
1½ tsp baking powder
1 tsp vanilla
100ml milk
100ml milk
1 tspn pure vanilla essence

1 Preheat the oven to 175°C. Grease and flour a 20cm Bundt tin.
2 Beat the sugar and eggs together until light and fluffy.

3 Melt the butter and add the milk to it .

4 Add the butter and milk mixture to the sugar and egg and beat again.

5 Sift together flour and baking powder and add this to the egg, butter and milk mix. Blend well. Add vanilla essence and mix in gently.

6 Put into prepared Bundt tin (grease and lightly flour the tin) and bake for 30 to 40 minutes.

SERVES 6–8

En route home, stopping off in LA, I had a bad hotel breakfast. Never to be repeated, it gave me a lasting memory of the United States. Jet-lagged and confused, stupidly I had gone to bed even though it was 11 am local time. I had already breakfasted on the flight from London many hours earlier and I should have been eating an early lunch. Instead, something enticed me to order the full American breakfast, a decision I regretted for the next twelve hours. Pancakes, syrup, bacon, fruit—mountains of food. Everything was supersized, as many American food experiences are.

Many years later, ordering a pasta dish in a small northwest American town—we had chosen a more upmarket-looking Italian place to try and avoid the usual mountain of food—the pasta arrived and it was beautiful, but more enormous than ever. I found out later that there were the equivalent of thirteen servings on my plate. I could have shared it with twelve friends and we would all have been well fed. Why? Why? Why?

My final memory of that first trip was, however, extraordinary and positive. I will never forget standing inside the crater of

Haleakala on the Island of Maui in the Hawaiian group. It was dawn at 3000 metres above sea level and it was freezing cold, but we breakfasted on delicious fresh mango and yoghurt. This was a good memory as we looked south and turned to head for home.

CHAPTER 8

A taste of Italy at home

In the late 1980s social and eating activities became more challenging on the home front as our expectations and tastes broadened. My daughter was leaving for London and was convinced a special dinner would help calm us all. The dinner was served—prosciutto and melon to begin, with rosemary flatbread, followed by clams steamed in white wine, veal in cream with mushrooms, sole baked in white wine with fresh gooseberry sauce, a fricassa de fungi, and pollo arosto alla tarragone. I look back at that menu in amazement. How did we ever find the time to prepare such food?

Pollo arosto alla tarragone

This makes a wonderful hot or cold dish for a summer outdoor table or picnic.

1 whole chicken (I like to use free range)
1 lemon
55g butter

salt and pepper
1 bunch fresh tarragon
1 tbspn chopped fresh tarragon, extra

1 Preheat the over to 180°C. Rub the outside of the chicken with the 2 halves of a cut lemon.
2 Mash together the butter, salt, pepper and chopped tarragon leaves (and stalks if tender) from the bunch.
3 Place this mixture inside the chicken.
4 Place the chicken in a covered baking dish and bake until the chicken is cooked.
5 Leave it to cool in the resulting liquid (the stock).
6 Take the chicken out of the liquid, drain and reserve the stock, then place the chicken on a serving dish.

SERVES 4

I often make another version of pollo arosto alla tarragone, using coconut cream. Prepare as with the previous dish but after placing the chicken stuffed with the butter tarragon mixture into a small baking dish, make incisions under the skin on the breasts and thighs of the chicken.

Take a can of coconut cream and spoon at least 2 tbspn of the coconut cream into each incision. Pour the remainder into the chicken cavity and over the top. Also pour a little olive oil over the bird and plenty of salt and pepper. Place tinfoil over the chicken. Cook at 190°C for 1 hour, taking the tinfoil off after about 20 minutes. This is a tasty, moist flavoursome chicken dish and remains a family favourite.

The Italian influence definitely had an impact back home in New Zealand. On my return, passion and colour and confidence abounded. When ten of us got together to celebrate a friend's late-spring birthday, I made fresh strawberry ice cream, raspberry fool (see page 192) and a special chocolate cake with Drambuie icing. We finished the meal with coffee and mints. What a feast—excess in all directions.

Strawberry ice cream (Rosie's version)

After much experimentation with both the recipes of Elizabeth David and Nigella Lawson I have come up with the following fairly easy version. It meets with approval on most occasions.

500g fresh strawberries
110g sugar plus 2 tbsp extra
2 eggs, separated
400ml cream
2 drops vanilla essence
1 tbsp lemon juice

1 Hull and chop the strawberries.
2 Put in a bowl and sprinkle with the 2 tablespoons of sugar.
3 Beat the egg yolks with the sugar until they are thick and pale yellow.
4 Beat the egg whites in a separate bowl until they have stiff peaks.
5 In another bowl beat the cream and vanilla until soft peaks form.
6 Puree the strawberry pieces in the food processor and add the lemon juice.
7 Now take all ingredients and fold in together.

8 Pour into two 1l containers for freezing. Cover either with a lid or cling film.

9 While this ice cream is in the freezer it is important to take out and gently stir about every 3 hours. This ensures a creamy texture and also the full integration of the strawberries, which will otherwise tend to drop to the bottom of the container.

MAKES 2 LITRES.

That year there are pre-Christmas memories of cherries being picked, boats being sanded in the bottom paddock and children in all directions, especially up the walnut trees. 'Trust, loyalty and tolerance.' That's what the elderly local man told me at the beach during that summer in the Bay. 'That's what you need in order to have a successful and long-lasting relationship.' He should know—he and his wife had made it through 55 years of married life.

Once again, a new decade brought with it a different way of doing things. European and other travel adventures continued to influence the preparation of food for us as a family and for our travelling friends back in New Zealand. After a journey, it is a gift I can give others, sharing the treasures from my travels as I make delicious new food for my friends and family back home.

In 1990, I learnt to make a galette of tomato and aubergine, and it is still a favourite. Then, too, I discovered sorbets, another favourite, especially when our wild blackberries are ripe for the picking. Sorbets have been served as a dessert in Italy since Roman times when snow was collected and brought back to the cities, where it was sweetened and flavoured with lemon juice. We had brought a taste of Italy to Governors Bay.

Tomato and aubergine galette

I serve this as an entrée or vegetarian main.

2–4 aubergines
8 tbspn olive oil
1 clove garlic, crushed
1 medium onion, minced or finely chopped
500g ripe tomatoes, skinned, deseeded and chopped
   (or 2 × 400g cans chopped tomato)
salt and freshly ground black pepper
250g unsweetened Greek-style yoghurt

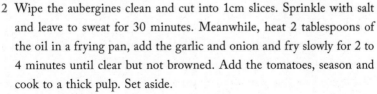

1 Preheat the oven to 180°C.
2 Wipe the aubergines clean and cut into 1cm slices. Sprinkle with salt and leave to sweat for 30 minutes. Meanwhile, heat 2 tablespoons of the oil in a frying pan, add the garlic and onion and fry slowly for 2 to 4 minutes until clear but not browned. Add the tomatoes, season and cook to a thick pulp. Set aside.
3 Fry the aubergine slices in batches in the remaining oil, until they turn a golden brown.
4 Arrange a layer of aubergine slices on the bottom of an oval or rectangular ceramic dish with deep sides.
5 Spread with a little tomato pulp and a little yoghurt.
6 Continue to layer the aubergine, yoghurt and tomato pulp, finishing with a layer of aubergine.

7 Cover the galette with tinfoil, pressing down lightly, and bake for 40 to 45 minutes.

8 Cool the galette in the dish for a few minutes.

9 Serve in slices and if you have any of the tomato pulp mixture left, pour it over the galette at the time of serving.

SERVES 6

Blackberry granita

You are aiming for crunchy pieces of granita rather than a frozen slab so take the time to break it up as crystals form during the freezing process.

450g blackberries
100g sugar
175ml water
few leaves of apple mint or rose geranium

1 Crush the blackberries and pass the pulp through a sieve to get rid of the seeds.

2 Heat the sugar and water to make a syrup and add whole leaves of apple mint or rose geranium and set aside to cool.

3 Strain the syrup, add to the sieved pulp and place in freezing trays.

4 Stir and break up the granita every 2 to 3 hours as it is freezing. Best eaten within two days while the flavours are strong.

The 1990s were turbulent times with our children. They were growing up and we all tossed around together, everyone battling for their own space. Dealing with adolescents in the household and large scale projects at work put pressure on the relationship front and, for once, not even cooking could make me feel better.

How are we, the baby-boomer generation, passing on the values we have been developing around lifestyle and food preparation to our children? I have three children and they all cook to a greater or lesser degree, but one showed a great interest in the preparation and presentation of food from an early age. No moderation for this boy. He went full-on into this interest with a passion and minimal tuition. It was all instinct and observation but, unfortunately, economics was never his thing.

I remember a particular occasion that brought this message home. It was an evening mid-week. The grocery shopping in those days was done fortnightly—driven by economy and time saving. The 'shop' had been done the day before, so there was plenty of food in the house. He, the teenage son, was at home and we, the parents, were working late. We told him we would be home around eight-thirtyish, possibly as late as nine, and not to worry about a meal for us. 'Just make yourself and your brother something and we'll get a takeaway.' He muttered something like, 'Don't worry, I'll cook . . .' but in all the busyness of my day his comment was completely forgotten.

I filled up on hot chips and a Thai takeaway, and it was about nine when we arrived home. The dining room and kitchen were brightly lit, the kitchen windows all steamed up. As I descended the steps from the garage to the house, I could see the table was fully extended and set for four. As I got closer I saw it was 'groaning' with steaming platters of food and, right in the middle, a stuffed whole chicken, beautifully arranged, and a bowl with a mountain of buttered carrots, another of potatoes and another of button mushrooms. It was like the dining scene from the movie *Babette's Feast*, a popular Danish film released in 1987.

I was beside myself—it looked as if he had used a whole week's groceries for one meal and, worse than that, how could I do it justice when I'd just filled up on takeaways? I had to be gracious. After all, how many mothers could come home to this sort of feast prepared by their 15-year-old son on a mid-week school night?

Stuffed roast chicken (Babette style)

Here is a version I have used in more recent years. Everyone loves this stuffing and it helps keep the bird very moist. It can also be used with great success as a stuffing for the Christmas turkey and it's gluten free.

For the stuffing
1 cup cooked basmati rice
½ cup raisins or dried cranberries
chopped parsley, to taste
2 tbspn finely chopped rosemary
55g butter
zest of 1 lemon (retain the lemon)
1 egg
1 onion, finely chopped
1 tspn white wine or chicken stock
½ cup fresh walnuts (or almonds), chopped
finely chopped spicy salami (optional)

1 size-16 free-range chicken
olive oil
salt and pepper

1 Preheat the oven to 180°C.
2 Mix all the stuffing ingredients together, using more chicken stock if it is not moist enough.
3 Cut the zested lemon in half and rub the cut edge all over the chicken.
4 Place the stuffing mixture inside the chicken cavity. If there is extra stuffing mixture, put it in a small ovenproof dish and bake.
5 Pour a few tablespoons of olive oil over the bird after it has been placed in the roasting dish and season with salt and pepper. Bake for at least 2 hours until the chicken is cooked.

SERVES 6

CHAPTER 9

Flavours of the Pacific

For many New Zealanders, the Pacific Islands are a great spot for a winter holiday to warm up when the going gets tough. The recipe for one of my favourite fish dishes is the best thing I brought back from a family visit to an island in the Fiji group. Malololeilei fish, named after the island we stayed on and where the dish is served as a local specialty, always triggers memories of warmth, freedom, risk-taking and passion.

For an escape from winter down-under, Fiji certainly gives those of us lucky enough to visit there in our winter the warm temperatures that we normally experience in summer at home. There are safe harbours, clear water, laid-back island culture and music, and a very different cuisine that includes taro, long thin green beans, whole pigs roasting on a spit, the freshest fish you'll get anywhere, coconut and always bananas. There are lots of coconuts and they are used in many dishes and prepared in all sorts of different ways.

Malololeilei fish is a simple dish made with the catch of the day—often you can purchase this on the beach—and coconut from the palms that fringe the beaches. In Fiji, it is most likely made with mahi mahi or wahoo—both dense, thick white-fleshed fish—but home in New Zealand any firm white-fleshed fish, such as blue cod, monkfish, warehou or hapuku, will be just as good as long as it is fresh from the sea.

Malololeilei fish

In Fiji, this is made with cream fresh from the coconut, but a can of coconut cream or milk will work as well. This dish can be accompanied by mango and wedges of freshly cut pineapple, if available, for added tropical flavour.

butter
oil
2 onions, sliced into rings
2–4 large tomatoes, cut into pieces
2–4 fillets of fresh fish, cut into large chunks
400ml coconut cream
salt and pepper

1 Heat the butter and oil in an ovenproof dish or heavy-based pan and gently fry the onions and tomatoes. When softened, add the fish pieces, taking care not to cook too much.
2 Pour over the coconut cream and season to taste.
3 Place the lid on the pan and allow to cook either on an element or in the oven for 10 to 15 minutes until the fish is cooked.

SERVES 4

I have made many versions of this fish dish, but none has tasted quite as good as the first time we had it on the beautiful island of Malololeilei where, eating at dusk, the warmth of the day's hot sun, the lullaby of the lapping sea and island music sung by the locals—so slow and melodic—mixes with the simple flavours of this dish to wash away all the cares of your other, stay-at-home world.

I also have great memories of dining on spit-roasted pig, anticipated all day by the enticing aroma of the pig slowly cooking over the hot embers of a pit fire. The crackling is highly sought after and exciting to bite into. It's no wonder this place where the warmth of the locals is legendary has long been a haven for sailors. Bula, bula!

Rarotonga, the largest island of the Cook Islands, is another Pacific neighbour close enough for easy holidays from New Zealand. When we visited, we were amused by the antics of an overweight, white-haired, white-bearded American gent who looked a lot like Father Christmas—Raymond Briggs's Father Christmas on a hot holiday. We were dining in the same small Rarotongan restaurant where he loudly ordered a steak for main and pecan pie for dessert.

His steak had been received, but it was not the huge slab of meat Americans are used to and it was hidden from view under a salad, with some mushrooms on the side. He searched briefly for the meat which was beneath the mushrooms, but failed to find it. He nibbled at the salad, pushed the mushrooms to one side and then sat and waited for his steak to arrive. His plate was removed and then another arrived. His indignation was loud when instead of a large juicy steak he was served pecan pie. 'Where's my steak? I ordered steak and this is pecan pie.'

Meat is in limited supply in Rarotonga and, therefore, very expensive. There was little sympathy for this man at the corner table who had just sent his uneaten steak back to the kitchen. That also helps to explain why New Zealanders on holiday often take a suitcase of frozen meat if they are staying in self-catered accommodation in the Cooks. As you can imagine, the combination of flight delays and hot tropical temperatures can make for some interesting contents when suitcases go astray!

As always, I took home ideas for adapting tried-and-true recipes with the flavours of the Pacific.

In 1994 we were in Kororareka, Russell, in the Bay of Islands, en route to a wonderful hideaway. Whangaruru is a place of peace, lush native bush, remote beaches and huge ancient pohutukawa trees. Up the hill is the site of an ancient Maori pa that has a magnificent 360 degree view of all possible enemy advances. Further around the bays we reached House Bay in time to watch the sun go down. We had our aperitifs sitting on the beach—wines, beers, cheeses, olives, biscuits—and dug for pipi. The small tasty shellfish are easily dug from the sand at the water's edge at low tide. The sun went down and we made our way, eight or more of us, over the headland carrying a bag of pipi back to the bach to prepare dinner. The first course, a wonderful hotpot of pipi, cockles and tuatua, cooked outside over the open fire, was created from all local ingredients.

Shellfish hotpot

This is a wonderful simple dish to share on a summer evening around an open fire and it can be made in any quantity, depending on the day's harvest and the number of people you need to feed.

2 fennel bulbs, sliced, or 1 small onion, diced
2 cloves garlic
1 sprig of rosemary
2 cups dry white wine
1–2kg mixed shellfish (at the Te Pipi homestead our friend Sarah used pipi,
*   tua tua and cockles)*

1 Place the fennel or onion, garlic, rosemary and wine into a large lidded pot you are happy to use over an outdoor fire and heat gently.
2 Add the well-washed shellfish in batches, according to size. Put the lid on and put the pot back onto the full heat of the fire. Each batch should take about 5 minutes or so before the shells open and are ready for eating. Discard any shellfish that don't open and serve the cooked shellfish on a platter with some of the cooking juices and some crusty bread to mop them up.

SERVES 4–6 AS AN ENTRÉE

This was followed by ratatouille, potato and fresh beans from our hostess and, like the entrée, it was eaten outdoors under the starry sky, until biting insects and dropping temperatures drove us inside.

For dessert, fresh peach ice cream was followed by coffee and chocolate. Carrying the warmth of sunshine and friendship from this place in the north of New Zealand, we are reminded there's a good life to be had here following our own traditions close to home.

Fresh peach ice cream

This is made with puréed fresh peaches but other fruit can be substituted.

500g fresh white-fleshed peaches, destoned
85g sugar
2 tbspn water
125ml cream, whipped

1 Simmer the peaches in the 2 tablespoons of water over a medium heat, until just softened.
2 Drain, retaining the liquid. Remove the skins and pulp or mash the fruit and set aside to cool.
3 Simmer the sugar and the retained peach cooking liquid together for a few minutes and set aside to cool.
4 Fold the fruit, syrup and whipped cream together and spread the mixture into a freezer proof container with a lid.
5 Stir twice during the freezing process, which should take 2-3 hours.

SERVES 4–6

CHAPTER 10

Hungry for life

First there was the daughter who had gone to live in London. Later in the decade a son went to school in France and, later still, another son left for Europe to wander about for some years. Mark and I also made frequent trips to Europe throughout the 1990s. We visited many new places and there was an explosion of new experiences. As we savoured what the world had on offer, my friend Sarah and I stored away ideas that appealed, jotting down ingredients and methods along with sketches, photographs and diary entries. We brought them all home. It is a time of acceleration of new experiences on all fronts, of a great richness and variety, both in our home lives, our working lives and our travelling lives. Here is a diary note from these times.

> Lake District—Long View—dressed for dinner! It was a Bank Holiday in the UK so it hadn't been easy to find accommodation for five in the heart of the Lake District. We finally took the only place on offer even though it was way outside our usual price range. Hey, it was just one night, and it would give us a different view of the UK tourist industry. Rural delight and a beautiful setting, Beatrix Potter country and a solid, heavy-timbered home. We climbed the stairs and

delighted in the low ceilinged dark-wood interior of our bedroom. We pulled from our bags the best clothes we had with us—crumpled but able to be sorted. Dinner was at 7 pm, and be dressed for it was the instruction, a tie please for the gentlemen. Well, this posed a bit of a problem, but two ties were found in husband Mark's bag, he had needed them for meetings in London earlier, one for him and one for Philip, but what about the teenage son travelling with us? No decent trousers let alone a tie. He was determined to try his chances tie-less so we made our way as confidently as we could, down the stairs towards the dining room.

Enroute, noticing in the stairwell perched on the railings, some unusual decorations, like oversized 'hackeysacks', but in animal shapes, they slouched over the railings.

We made it into the pre-dinner drinks area of the dining room full of chatting guests, all British it seemed, where sherry was being served. Before we made it to the drinks, a discreet intervention from our host. 'I'm afraid your son must wear a jacket and a tie for dinner madam.'

Our son was not to be stopped by this request (the same son who had been evicted from Harrods for wearing jeans—jeans that hung down below the bum and collected holes at ground level as was the fashion at the time). He disappeared briefly and returned with a neck piece—you couldn't call it a tie—but indeed it did wrap around his neck. A large pink mouse. A new use for the bean-bag stuffed animals on the stairwell. Our host was not amused but managed to maintain his decorum and went on to serve a very delicious meal.

Another lasting memory was from an altogether different trip, to the Three Ways House Hotel, home of the famous Pudding Club in the heart of the English countryside, in a little village in the

Cotswolds. The waitress, when asked about the Pudding Club, answered, 'It's very popular, madam, people are booked up to six months ahead. Ten puddings are supplied and people taste each one . . . there are special rooms named after the different puddings.' I was relieved we were not part of the club requiring the tasting of ten puddings and could order just one with our meal, and to note also that membership of this club accounted for the name on the door near my room—the Spotted Dick Room. My travel companion and I let our minds run riot and only just managed to control our mirth as the waitress left our table, looking most perturbed. Still, that night we enjoyed a real summer pudding with fresh berries. It was a wonderful way to end a day of garden visits, bombarding the olfactory senses with the scents of rose. Later, I resisted the temptation to add the steamed golden-syrup pudding bodywash to my bath despite encouragement from the girl at the front desk telling me how wonderful it was to be able to indulge in the aroma of a favourite pudding while lying in a bath knowing you weren't gaining a single gram!

After the Cotswolds we went to Paris, where I celebrated another birthday. I remember cramped and noisy accommodation, as well as a full moon and some memorable meals, including a wonderful lunch on the Boulevard Saint-Germain. Treats that day included rum baba and a delightful waiter. 'Paris makes me feel so much alive, so much a woman,' I commented in my diary. I'm sure I wouldn't be the first woman to write that, or the last.

I contemplate why I find Paris so fascinating. There are lots of reasons—the women, their utter ease in dressing and the elegant way they walk down the street, the eccentricity of local dog lovers (we saw dogs in handbags, dogs on bikes, dogs on the laps of people in wheelchairs, dogs on shop benches, pampered dogs, super-clean dogs with pink pink skin shining through their over-shampooed glistening curls to name a few).

But it is the food, always the food, that takes me back to Paris. Through the years I have often found myself eating alone on my travels and I'm determined not to miss out on the gorgeous eating experiences available just because I am alone. I have practised the art of booking and going to a good restaurant, taking time to savour my meal and of not feeling embarrassed because I'm alone. These lone dining experiences are certainly a way of heightening observations of others around you

The days are filled with the joys of Paris—visits to the Musée de l'Orangerie, the Musée d'Orsay, the Tuileries Gardens, Sainte-Chappelle, concerts, climbing to the top of the tower at Notre Dame. Dinner with friends and sitting on a roof terrace watching the light shift over the city . . . Sacré-Coeur, the luminous light white–grey building standing out against the dark grey sky behind.

Another day spent consuming rich experiences—a hairdresser enjoying his craft, sculpting my hair, leaving it sleek and full of bounce. Confident with my new Parisian appearance, I head in search of a good coq au vin. 'It must have been a grand coq to supply the meat for these bones,' I commented in my diary. It tasted so good—it was the real thing made with meat from a large cockerel.

And for dessert to follow, what could possibly beat a tarte aux poires, with its delicate shortcrust pastry that melted in the mouth and tree-ripened pears tasting of autumn and the countryside? I am left wondering how I will ever cook again upon my return home, but I do, and the fruits of my labour are even better than before.

Tarte aux poires

I use Doyenne du Comice pears, but this can also be made with apples. Start by making a blind-baked sweet short pastry shell. For this tart the shell needs to be cooked for about 5 minutes longer than for the Tarte aux mures (see page 55).

1 sweet short pastry shell (see Sweet short pastry, page 55)

For the fruit filling
5 firm pears, peeled, cored and sliced
55g sugar
½ tspn cinnamon

For the custard filling
1 egg
55g sugar
30g sifted flour
125ml cream
icing sugar

1 Preheat the oven to 170°C.
2 Place the pear slices, sugar and cinnamon in a bowl and toss gently to coat the pear slices.
3 Arrange the pear slices in the pastry shell and bake for 20 to 30 minutes, until they look tender.
4 Meanwhile, make the custard. Beat the egg and sugar together until thick and creamy.
5 Add the flour and cream and whisk until smooth.
6 Pour the custard over the pears and put back in the oven for about 10 minutes.

7 Take from the oven and sprinkle heavily with icing sugar.

8 Return to the oven until browned on top and when the tart is tested
the skewer comes out clean.

SERVES 6–8

***

One day, my friend and I had a competition with each other to
write a poem explaining, 'Why Paris?' The winner had their meal
paid for that night. Here's my winning poem!

Why Paris?
I came to be fed
Hungry for life
I came
Tears a surprise
As life slipped back in
Sapphire bullets of pure joy
Direct to the heart
Paris has breathed on me.

Once again, I have to leave Europe and, once again, my hunger
for life has been well fed.

CHAPTER 11

Turkish delights

In 1997 my husband and I visited Antalya in the south of Turkey, for a World Forestry Congress. The city is often described as the Turkish Riviera. The beach down the cliff in front of our hotel was a peaceful spot in an otherwise stressful environment—the temperatures were very hot! It was hard to believe the hassling going on in the streets, and I quickly realised I had a lot to learn. I had spent the day, as many do, trying to negotiate a deal on a carpet. After many cups of apple tea, many pieces of Turkish delight, many glasses of cola, a lot of talk and sweaty negotiations, I was still unsure as to whether or not I had a good deal.

Memorable events in Turkey are numerous, but the food remains uninspiring for me with the exception of the breakfasts, which were delicious. Our pink hotel, Tütav Türk Evi Otelleri, small and exquisite, was perched on a cliff overlooking the Mediterranean with a backdrop of mountains shrouded in cloud. The courtyard where we dined was an oasis of calm, with a tree in the centre. Yoghurt and dried apricots plumped up after an overnight soaking, fetta cheese, without any goaty taste, and bread—soft, white and freshly baked—with tasty green and black olives. Then more bread, sweet this time, with fetta and jam accompanied by apple tea, Turkish tea or coffee. Sometimes there was also a boiled egg.

Following some difficult negotiations with the captain of a local boat one night on the waterfront, Mark and I had organised a dinner cruise for some people from the congress for the following night. It was to include a visit to a waterfall further along the coast. We put the word about and at 8 pm the next evening 21 people from nine different countries turned up at our hotel ready to go. They were a mixed bunch. With so many strong personalities and different languages and high expectations, as the organisers we were feeling stressed by the time we boarded the boat. Everyone clambered up to the top deck. The alcohol flowed and the singing started, mixing with the chatter of many languages, the overly loud taped Turkish music and the engine noise from the boat.

As we pulled out from the shelter of the harbour, the boat began to roll. We all moved to the lower deck but the roll was still bad enough to make some people sick. No more singing and the drinking certainly slowed down. The biggest disaster though was still to come—the prepaid dinner. We had become accustomed to a daily fare of fish, tomato paste and rice in different forms, but this meal had the additional problem of being cold. Cold fish, cold chicken and plain tomato paste, instead of the tasty sauces we had previously enjoyed. I don't think there was a chef on board at all.

The food memory of that night is bad but what took place where we were trying to eat it was even more memorable in a bad way. We had motored to the waterfall, which admittedly was spectacular, and moored so dinner could be served. We had been looking forward to a peaceful moonlit night on the water, but peace there was not. Numerous low-flying aeroplanes roared overhead—we seemed to be moored directly under a flight path to Antalya Airport and, worse, in front of a military establishment. Army personnel took exception to our mooring site and a delegation arrived by boat and swarmed up rope ladders onto our boat. We heard heated discussions with the captain and crew before they left, and off we went as well to a new mooring. Thankfully, the atrocious dinner was forgotten in all the drama.

However, I will always remember the pink hotel and its perfect breakfasts. Sitting there, in the courtyard, open to the sky and looking out on the clear green Mediterranean, with mountains rising from the mist beyond, was a glimpse of paradise. Here is a typical Turkish fish and tomato dish, and it's the one I wish we had been served that night by the waterfall.

Soganli domatesli balik

This simple dish is served even in upmarket restaurants in Turkey.

500g red mullet or similar
1 tbspn olive oil
salt and pepper
2 onions, sliced into rings
6 fresh tomatoes, chopped or 2 × 400g
    cans chopped tomatoes
1 tbspn tomato paste
4 bay leaves
2 lemons, cut into wedges

1 Preheat the oven to 100°C. Place the fish in an earthenware or other baking dish.
2 Dribble the olive oil over the fish and season with salt and pepper.
3 Spread the onion rings, tomato pieces, tomato paste and bay leaves over the fish.
4 Cover with tinfoil and bake for 20 to 30 minutes.
5 Serve with lemon wedges.

SERVES 4

CHAPTER 12

Travel at all costs

As we and all our friends were concentrating more on careers and less on home-making throughout the 1990s, eating out became more frequent. We continued to pursue contentment and happiness although for some of us it seemed to be pretty elusive. Some of us came close to the abyss of separation in our relationships, and then recovered to move forward again. Once again, even the worst moments of despair were lightened by a shared tasty meal. We ate pappa al pomodoro and Italian flat bread, followed by zabaglione and amaretti biscuits, with plenty of bubbly and good red wine. It's amazing what a mid-winter dinner with friends can do, in the midst of relationship dramas, to lift spirits when you think your world is falling apart.

Italian flat bread with rosemary

(Adapted from Lorenza De'Medici's *Italy the Beautiful Cook Book*.)

Everyone loves this bread, especially children—which now includes my grandchildren. I like to use Maldon sea salt, but there are many more coarse salts available now that would add a different flavour.

15g fresh yeast (or 2 heaped tbspn dried yeast)
125ml warm water
4–5 cups all-purpose plain flour (plus extra for kneading)
3 tbspn extra virgin olive oil
2–3 large sprigs fresh rosemary
coarse sea salt

1 Dissolve the yeast in the warm water and let stand for 10 minutes in a covered bowl, or until it shows some activity and begins to bubble.
2 Put the flour in another bowl and make a well in the centre.
3 Pour in the dissolved yeast mixture, then mix together gently, adding enough water to make a soft dough.
4 Leave to rise for 20 minutes in a warm place. Sometimes, I do this on the top of the stove when the oven has been on or, best of all, cover the bowl with a cloth and set it beside the wood burner.
5 When the mixture has more than doubled in size add the extra flour (about ½ cup) and mix until a dough forms.
6 Knead the dough until very smooth and elastic, at least 10 minutes. Form it into a ball. Leave in the covered bowl to rise again until it has almost doubled in size.
7 Preheat the oven to 230°C.
8 Knead the dough again briefly. Roll out on a lightly floured board.

9 Brush a large shallow baking tin with oil.
10 Push the dough down into the baking tin with your fingers until it is about 1cm thick.
11 Indent the risen dough quickly with your fingertips.
12 Brush the top with olive oil then sprinkle with the rosemary and coarse salt.
13 Let the dough rise again for 15 to 20 minutes.
14 Bake for 15 minutes or until a light golden colour. When cooked turn out of the baking tin immediately and allow to cool slightly before cutting and serving warm.

SERVES 8–10

Pappa al pomodoro

A thick and tasty soup that Italians stress must be made from the best products, especially the bread and the oil.

250ml extra virgin olive oil
½ cup fresh torn sage leaves
3-4 chopped garlic cloves
250g stale bread, finely sliced (a heavy sourdough is good to use)
salt and freshly ground pepper
1kg peeled tomatoes, fresh or canned
2 litres chicken, beef or vegetable stock

1 Heat the oil in a heavy-based saucepan and add the sage and garlic. Cook until the garlic begins to colour.
2 Add the finely sliced bread and brown all pieces on both sides. Season with salt and pepper.

3 Pulp the tomatoes in a food processor and add to the bread mixture, continuing to simmer the mixture.
4 In a separate saucepan bring the stock to the boil then add to the tomato mixture.
5 Reduce the heat and continue to simmer the soup for at least another 40 minutes.

SERVES 4–6

Zabaglione

This is a good basic zabaglione recipe, to which you can add fruit when serving.

6 egg yolks
6 half eggshells caster sugar
6 half eggshells marsala
1 egg white

1 Whisk the egg yolks with the sugar in the top of a double boiler until frothy.
2 Stir in the marsala and whisk until the mixture is very thick and doubles in volume.
3 Remove from the heat and keep beating until the mixture has cooled.
4 In a separate bowl, beat the egg white until stiff and fold into the yolk mixture.
5 Transfer the zabaglione to a serving dish or individual dishes and serve warm.

SERVES 6

Grape jelly infused strawberries

This simple strawberry dessert goes very well with zabaglione.

300g strawberries, hulled and cut into pieces
juice of 1 orange
1 tbspn grape jelly

1 Place everything in a small bowl and leave to soak for an hour before serving.

SERVES 6

In my work as a theatre director I have an exercise designed to sort out the students according to their level of spontaneity. I ask them to make a straight line facing towards the front, single file. Then I ask them to place themselves according to their own perception of themselves, indicating one end is 'I am a very spontaneous person and along with this can often go trouble with a capital T' and the other end is 'I am a planner, so organised that sometimes I prevent myself from going forward in life because of the severity of my need to plan'. Along the continuum between are various combinations of the two, and in some cases a person may have to walk back and forth while they ponder the mix of their ability to be spontaneous balanced with being a planner. When I was first asked to do this exercise I was one of the latter—pacing indecisively up and down the full length of the line.

The desire for travel and new experience is so powerful that for me it confounds all reason, i.e., funds. The planner-me hatches the plan then, without too much notice, the spontaneous-me puts it into action. Then the rationalisation process comes to the fore, blocking all the nagging doubts that creep in. 'How will you get the money?' 'How will you pay it back?' 'Who will mind the family? the business?' It all fades into temporary insignificance as the latest plan hatches. And once again, I'm off!

The airline privilege from my sister allowing me to travel at ridiculously low prices came with some restrictions, which included travelling at short notice and a need to be able to adapt quickly to changes in destination, dates of arrival and departure times. Once I'd accepted these limitations, the unexpected changes and delays became another part of the adventure. Heading out into the relative unknown, I loved the opportunities this provided, and unlike many families of airline staff I made good use of the perk, extending my work repertoire and my palate. These journeys took me to some unusual destinations, fulfilling a variety of objectives. Work-related experiences and food experiences along the way extended my world and left me with many rewarding memories to sustain me when I got home.

One night in New York the two strands of my interests came together as I enjoyed a pre-theatre meal at the Divine Bar on 51st Street. I ate an omelette, alone, and its bejewelled appearance—thanks to golden caviar—was something to behold. Outside, a black sultry sky finally triggered an electrical storm and a deluge of huge raindrops. After the brilliant two-woman play, 'Collected Stories' by Donald Margulies, a highlight of the night was meeting a much-admired actress and writer, Uta Hagen, whose book *Respect for Acting* was a teaching bible for me. She was small and fragile but feisty, with a long cigarette holder in one hand and small dog under her other arm. She had a rich, gravelly voice. Now, I look at the orange porcelain teapot, bought from the retired ballet dancer who sat in his small, packed antique shop opposite the theatre (that I subsequently carried around the globe for many weeks) and remember that night.

I also went to the UK and then on to South Africa, visiting my old friend Paula in Johannesburg. The highlight was our trip to Madagascar. It's a four-hour flight east from Johannesburg, across the straits, and our hosts were people I had met with Mark in Antalya in Turkey. They lived in Antananarivo. The name enthralled me—Antananarivo, Madagascar. I had always had a fascination for the islands to the east of Africa—Madagascar, Reunion and the Seychelles.

The invitation had been an open one, and here I was in this part of the world. I might never have another chance of travelling to the island, especially with such a good friend who had lived in Africa for the last decade.

Madagascar is described by many as a world apart—some people call it the world's best kept secret. I was certainly constantly surprised. Our hosts, Nivo and Raj, were so welcoming. She was a dentist in the mornings and a factory owner exporting beautiful hand-embroidered linen in the afternoons. He was a government official, the Minister of Forests and Oceans. Together they are also part-owners of a French restaurant where we dined on two occasions. This restaurant, Le Restaurant—Piano Bar, was another surprise in a city already full of surprises.

A place of magic and beauty hidden behind a high wall in an unlikely part of town, the restaurant was filled with joie de vivre, warmth and colour, and it served brilliant French cuisine. It was certainly different from the daily fare cooked by our hosts' native Malagasy home-help, which was an endless array of fairly tasteless rice or couscous with large chunks of indescribable meat and silverbeet-type green vegetables. I found all meat suspect after seeing the offerings hanging uncovered in the hot sun, covered by flies in abundance, at local meat vendors. I briefly wanted to be a vegetarian again.

Back in Johannesburg plans were made for a visit to Pilanesburg National Park, where we sat in a man-made hide, peering through wire mesh at the surrounding animals. We saw nine giraffes, three elephants (all bulls), herds of zebra and hundreds of monkeys, beautiful bird life and, of course, a wart hog on parade at the water hole where we 'whisperers' munched away on our picnic lunch. Chicken sandwiches, fresh peaches, cheeses—our hostess excelled herself in meal presentation, both at home and for the picnic. I also remember her preparing a memorable Nigerian stew for her other guest from Nigeria.

A good chicken sandwich

These are really tasty. I have never been much of a sandwich-maker, so I like this recipe because you don't have to be too perfect—which I'm not! It helps to use a very sharp knife to cut the sandwiches.

For the filling
1 chicken, poached
6 tbspn mayonnaise (see Sylvie's mayonnaise,
*   page 151, or use a good-quality purchased*
*   mayonnaise), plus extra for spreading*
1 stalk celery, finely chopped
1 tbspn salted baby capers
3 cloves garlic

2 tbspn chives
¼ cup freshly chopped parsley
16 slices white bread
washed fresh watercress to taste (optional)

1 Remove the breast meat from the poached chicken and shred.
2 Combine the shredded chicken with all the other filling ingredients.
3 Spread half the bread slices with some more of the mayonnaise, and if you have watercress leaves sprinkle these onto the bread slices.
4 Onto each slice of bread place 2 or 3 tablespoons of the chicken mixture and top with the remaining bread slices, resisting the temptation to put in too much.
5 Cut off the crusts and cut into 24 fingers or 32 squares or triangles.

SERVES 6–8

Nigerian chicken stew

I use Thai basil in this recipe. In Nigeria, it would be made with partminger, a herb that is part of the basil family and is sometimes called Nigerian curry leaf.

1 large chicken, cut into 10 portions
salt and pepper
1 tspn fresh thyme
570ml ground nut oil
2 large onions, sliced
225g fresh chillies
2 cloves garlic
1kg fresh tomatoes

1 small can tomato purée or ¼ tube tomato paste
2 tspn chopped Thai basil

1 Season the chicken pieces with the salt, pepper and thyme.
2 Heat the oil in a heavy-based frying pan large enough to hold all the chicken pieces and fry them until browned on both sides. Set them aside.
3 Fry the sliced onions, chillies and garlic until soft, then add the tomatoes and purée.
4 Finally, return the partially cooked chicken pieces to the pan, cover and continue cooking for 25 to 35 minutes until the chicken is cooked through.
5 Finally, stir in the chopped Thai basil. Serve with rice.

SERVES 6–8

Back in Johannesburg we visit the Gramadoelas Restaurant for dinner, widely known for its tradition of beautiful food, service and presentation. It is tasteful and welcoming, with a real African feel. I am already becoming used to the cars slowing at red lights but not stopping and our driver has become more vigilant at the lights as we get closer to the Market Theatre Laboratory, where I have been observing rehearsals during the days. Now we are heading back to Gramadoelas in the theatre complex.

Over pre-dinner drinks I begin to think about the craziness of post-apartheid South Africa 1998. Not the long-awaited dream of prosperity and equality for black South Africans but a disappointing, uncomfortable and disharmonious result for both the black and white population. The drive downtown has taken us into the heart of the old city but, instead of a humming centre, I see empty buildings and streets with aimless young people standing around sidewalk fires burning old rubber tyres.

'What's happened to the business district?' I ask. I'm told it has moved to the outskirts, nearer the tourist hotels. A trip to this restaurant, once so well attended for its international reputation—I see President Clinton's name in the guest pages along with other world celebrities—is now not for the faint hearted. My friend has organised another dinner guest, who will arrive separately. When she arrives she is distraught and dishevelled, minus her wallet and telephone. Not vigilant enough at the lights, she had become another victim of the common practice of wallet snatching. Thieves jump out at the car with a rock, smash the window, reach in and grab what they can from the car seat before running off. Our dinner that night was marred by her distress but the food was excellent.

I felt sad when I left the restaurant later that night; its impeccable reputation would probably not be enough to save it as people became too afraid to go 'downtown' after dark. Even so, years later as I write these lines I am shocked to learn that Gramadoelas has closed its doors after 45 years of famous company and fine food because of the murder of its co-founder.

My time in Africa was a blur of intense and mixed experiences of warmth and friendship, intermingled with a sense of fear and impotence to change things.

Chapter 13

Jam

It was autumn 1990 and there were flowers and fruit in abundance. Family, friends, lovers, good health and good food—it seemed idyllic. At the theatre, there was a new show for me to work on, an adaptation of the children's book *Jam*, written by Margaret Mahy, a much-loved author, fellow resident of Governors Bay and friend. The characters, Mr and Mrs Oberon, have a tree overflowing with plums and Mr O, who is a stay-at-home father, can't bear to see the plums go to waste, so he starts to make jam. He can't stop making jam and soon the house is overflowing with pots of plum jam. We had jam at the theatre, little people dressed as jam pots sitting in a hugely dangerous tree built on stage. We rehearsed daily.

And at home it was that time of year again—the season of mellow fruitfulness. So, when I arrived home there was more jam to be made from our own plums. And corn, tomatoes, blackberries, pumpkin, pears and apples were all in abundance and the air filled with the sound of chainsaws as people trimmed trees to give more winter light—this harsh sound is always an unwelcome accompaniment to an otherwise perfect season. The task of gathering in the produce was wonderfully satisfying. Late plums continued to ripen and fall from the trees faster than we could pick them and turn them into jam.

Best plum jam

This makes about 15 small jars of delicious jam.

2.7kg plums (I use Black Doris plums)
500ml water
2.3kg sugar

1 Wash and halve the plums and remove the stones, reserving about 12 stones. Crack and remove the kernels to cook with the plums.
2 Place the plums, kernels and water in a preserving pan and simmer gently for 45 minutes.
3 Place the sugar in a shallow dish and heat in a low oven for 10 minutes, but don't allow it to colour.
4 Remove the plums from the heat and add the warmed sugar. Mix well.
5 Return to the boil and cook over high heat until setting point is reached; this shouldn't take very long. Test for setting after 15 minutes by placing a spoonful of the hot jam onto a chilled saucer. Leave for a minute or two, then slowly draw a spoon through. If the mixture wrinkles and separates it is ready to set. If it stays runny it isn't, so boil for another 5 minutes and test again. Repeat at 5-minute intervals until the jam is ready to set.
6 Pour the hot jam into sterilised jam jars and seal.

The pain of see-sawing in relationship matters on the home front is eased by activities in the kitchen—preserving and laying down supplies for the winter. Good sense prevails as jams, jellies, sauces and pastes are made and a feeling of peace, warmth and security emanates through the house. Grape jelly, crabapple jelly, quince jelly, quince paste, tomato sauce, blackcurrant and Black Doris plum jams . . . they are all favourites then and now, twenty years on.

Crabapple jelly

If you use two-thirds of a preserving pan of crabapples you should get 10 to 12 small to medium-sized jars of jelly.

crabapples
water
sugar

1 Pick a quantity of ripe crabapples and place whole in a preserving pan.
2 Cover with water, bring to the boil and simmer until the fruit is tender.
3 Strain overnight through a jelly bag.
4 Next day, measure the liquid and gently heat in a pan.
5 Stir in 2 cups of sugar for every 2½ cups of liquid.
6 When dissolved, bring to the boil and keep boiling until setting point is reached. (See Best plum jam, page 107, for how to test for setting.)
7 Pour the hot jelly into sterilised jam jars and seal.

CHAPTER 14

Cora Lynn

The setting is the South Island of New Zealand, in the high country halfway between the east coast plains of Canterbury and the dramatic wilderness of the West Coast. High up, Cora Lynn Station, a 2400 hectare working farm, is nestled under the main-divide mountain ranges, the house surrounded by native beech forest. A group of us shared the lease on this wonderful mountain property for a number of years, retaining it until 1994 when the property was purchased and converted to its current use as a Wilderness Lodge. A place of retreat from our other lives, occupied on a time-share basis, this isolated high country house provided the setting for relaxation and revitalisation all year round. Whenever I think of Cora Lynn, I think of the aromas of manuka and pure mountain air, the pond frozen for skating in the winter and drowsy for paddling in summer, with insects buzzing overhead. Walks abounded in all directions, ideal for all levels of ability and energy. At the time this was the perfect setting for the wild young teenagers in our household. We would arrive with enough food for our stay, usually one or two weeks and, sometimes, during mid-summer, for longer. Roast meat was always a favourite in this appetite-enhancing mountain air.

Roast lamb, slow baked with cloves of garlic imbedded, sprinkled liberally with rock salt and rosemary brought from our Governors Bay home property, was a firm favourite. It quietly roasted away during the late afternoon and early evenings. For the walkers and the skiers returning from an afternoon of outdoor activity, the aroma was a wonderful welcome and an exciting promise of the evening meal to come.

One Sunday, during the winter school holidays, one of my sons developed bad asthma, more severe than usual. In the kitchen the roast was cooked, the veges not quite. The snow was deep and, as it was around 5 o'clock, dark was coming on fast. The nearest settlement was 20 minutes by car in one direction and the nearest medical help 35 to 40 minutes in the other direction. However, this meant negotiating a high mountain pass in terrible conditions, in the dark, and me the only adult. At least my car had snow chains. If we left to go for medical help we wouldn't come back until the snow melted. We would carry on to the coast and home. The decision required a rapid pack up and clearance of the kitchen, turning off the oven containing the delicious-smelling roast lamb and making sure the open fire was out. We weren't going to leave the roast behind. All the while the breathing of my nine-year-old son was becoming frighteningly laboured.

Things were thrown into the car—clothes, boots, bags, the dog. Hats, gloves and jackets were put on and the roast wrapped in foil and put into the back of the car. The boot was slammed down and we were on our way, slithering down the long drive, treacherous in these conditions, willing ourselves to reach the main road where the snow plough had been through. No longer exciting, as it had been earlier in the day, when the children had been towed along on their skis behind the car.

Finally, we made it to the main road and headed east through the sparkling white landscape, reassuring our patient we would reach the rural medical centre and a nebuliser soon.

Everyone was hungry. After all, we'd missed dinner and the car was steaming up with our combined breath and the heat from the leg of lamb. We were making fairly good time when a tyre blew, on an incline that would take us up to the highest point of the pass. It wasn't too dramatic, but I felt an increasing lack of control in the steering, in addition to the already testing icy conditions, as the tyre rapidly lost pressure. Here, the fourteen-year-old son came to the rescue. I couldn't have managed the tyre change in these conditions and on this incline without him. As we opened the boot to gather the tools and release the spare tyre, the sight of the still warm roast lamb was irresistible. While the tyre was changed and we tried to keep the breathless patient comfortable, the lamb was consumed. And, I have to say, I've never enjoyed a roast so much. No cutlery, no accompaniments. The patient even ate some.

Refuelled, we set off again and negotiated the pass with renewed confidence, making it to the other side and medical assistance, the plains, and eventually home, much later that night. Roast lamb preparation continues the same way today, winter and summer, whether it's to be roasted in the oven or baked on a barbecue. It never fails to please.

Mountain-style roast leg of lamb

Cook this with potatoes, kumara, yams, parsnips, pumpkin, butternut or a selection of veges—take your pick. You can also make lovely gravy at the end of the cooking process, using the roasting juices and your favourite gravy recipe, or simply serve this with grape jelly on the side.

1 lamb leg
12 cloves garlic
salt
sprigs of rosemary
oil
vegetables to roast, as available

1 Preheat the oven to 170°C.
2 Place the lamb leg in a good-sized baking dish, big enough to accommodate the vegetables alongside.
3 With a sharp knife make 12 incisions, spaced apart, into the meat.
4 Insert a clove of garlic into each incision.
5 Liberally salt the meat.
6 Cut pieces of rosemary and place on the meat and into the incisions with the garlic, if possible.
7 Drizzle oil over the surface of the meat and cover with tinfoil.
8 Cook the meat for 1 hour then remove the tinfoil. Add the vegetables and continue cooking for another hour or more, depending on the size of the leg. Baste the vegetables now and then so they brown evenly.

SERVES 6–8

CHAPTER 15

Winter and summer solstice

My work associated with theatre for young people continued to take me to some interesting places around the world, including a visit, in June 1999, to Tromsø, in the north of Norway. Five hundred delegates from over 40 countries gathered in this small town in the Arctic Circle—it's 70 degrees north. It was mid-summer solstice there and that meant 24-hour sunshine. While this was an amazing novelty for the visitors, it was an annual phenomenon for the locals. Even in mid-summer this tiny island appears stark, with a lot of snow still around the outer edge of town and on nearby hills. The houses are uniform and there are few signs of gardens as the leaves are just beginning to unfurl on the ubiquitous silver birches. More window boxes appeared daily, with nasturtiums, strawberries and flowering spring bulbs. It seems so wrong to me, to see daffodils and narcissus in mid-summer. Even in summer, seafood is an enormously important part of the local diet here. I was delighted to find delicious crustaceans that were truly super-sized on offer in local restaurants.

A wonderful feature of the local hotels was the practice of offering complementary hot food around 4.30 to 6.30 pm—it's probably essential for keeping spirits up on those 52 days of the year when daylight never comes.

By day, at the congress, we discuss theatre art as the universal expression of mankind and how it links large groups of the world's people—it is able to promote equality, peace, education and racial harmony. Theatre is a force for cultural unification. At this particular congress, we're looking at the rights of children to have leisure time, particularly in third-world countries. This is something children have in New Zealand as a birth right. By night, I explore the restaurants and cafés of Tromsø and climb the local mountain to share in the crazy, indulgent building of rock cairns and generally frolicking in the warm midnight sun.

Fish-eating experiences were many and varied, from the delicious catfish at Nord Frisken Restaurant to my least favourite—slices of whale meat with hard-boiled seagulls' eggs on the side. I was assured only one egg was taken from each seagull nest by the person collecting the eggs and that eating whale meat in this part of the world was not only okay but necessary. I still couldn't bring myself to try them.

I returned from Tromsø with a number of memories and mementos. The thing that was most difficult to carry, but has since given years of eating pleasure, was a heavy waffle iron. I also brought the waffle recipe with me, which has remained a family favourite. In Tromsø, waffles were eaten by locals and visitors on a daily basis—any excuse for a waffle. Arriving at a kiosk for a cup of coffee or tea, there would be the jar of waffle mix and bowls of jam and whipped cream on the counter. And of course the hot waffle irons ready to take the mix. They make a superb snack at any hour, giving much warmth and energy, probably as a result of the number of eggs in the mix.

Norwegian waffles

Have plenty of jam and whipped cream ready to add as a topping and hand these around as soon as they are cooked. The number of servings depends on how hungry everybody is. However, this batter will keep in the fridge for a few days to be used as required.

130g plain white flour
750ml–1 litre milk
pinch of salt
2 tbspn sugar
2 tspn baking powder
5 eggs
2 tspn oil

1 Put all the ingredients, including the oil, in a bowl and whisk until a smooth batter is formed. This mixture can be covered and left refrigerated for up to 2 days.
2 Heat and grease the waffle iron with butter. Pour on the waffle mixture in batches, taking care not to overfill the waffle iron.
3 Serve immediately or place the cooked waffles in a warm oven until ready to serve.

SERVES 4–6 (DEPENDING ON HOW HUNGRY YOU ARE!)

When I arrived back home, it's the winter solstice and it felt like a hard winter. I wondered if it's because I'm getting older and less tolerant of temperature extremes? How do we measure a hard winter? I heard someone a lot younger than me say, 'I miss the sun'. Maybe the absence of sunshine is the biggest challenge for us here in the long winter months. Of course, it's nothing compared to northern Norway but it's still a challenge.

The garden supplied its treats to the home table even in mid-winter. Flowering winter sweet is a delight, its delicate waxy blooms clinging to stark, almost-leafless winter branches, their heavenly scent bringing so much pleasure. The fragile pale-blue winter iris, stylosis, finds its way upwards and opens, sharing its beauty for a single day, despite rain, ice and even snow.

Inside, the offering of rich, orange pumpkin soup provided a positive note in an otherwise miserable mid-winter day. Pumpkin soup in all its variations, with some fine tuning, has survived all the eras, and all the fads—pumpkin soup has no pretensions. I remember American guests always being surprised by it. I think their use of this wonderfully versatile vegetable is restricted to the famous pumpkin pie, a Thanksgiving dessert, and Jack-o'-lantern decorations for Halloween.

Pumpkin and ginger soup

This is a delicious and comforting mid-winter soup. I use grey-skinned pumpkin for this—the kind that has deep-orange flesh.

1.2kg pumpkin
85g butter
2 tbspn oil
1 red onion, peeled and diced
2 cloves garlic, peeled and chopped
1 piece ginger, thumbsize, grated
grated nutmeg
pepper and salt
1 litre home-made chicken stock (or 1 tspn stock powder mixed with 1 litre water)

1 Skin the pumpkin and scoop out the seeds.
2 Chop into medium-sized pieces.
3 Melt the butter in a heavy-based saucepan and add the oil.
4 Cook the onion and garlic until lightly browned, stirring all the time.
5 Add the pumpkin pieces and stir-fry until they begin to change colour, but stop before they go brown.
6 Add the ginger, nutmeg and pepper and salt.
7 Pour in the chicken stock. Bring to a gentle simmer and continue to cook over a slow heat for at least 1 hour.
8 When all is soft either mash by hand, blend with a hand-held wand or put in a food processor and process to the desired texture.
9 Adjust seasoning before serving, if necessary.

SERVES 6

CHAPTER 16

Celebration

Across all eras and for all cultures, special food has been prepared when there is something to celebrate. Whether the celebration is a birthday, a wedding, a funeral, an anniversary, a religious holiday . . . whether it is self-catered, or prepared by caterers . . . in a restaurant or hired venue, people put a lot of effort into planning and preparing the food to be shared with others at a time of celebration.

Sometimes, we even take the brave, mad step of making our home the setting for a special family event. There have been birthdays and anniversaries, and parties just for the sake of having a party, but there had never been a wedding at Ribbonwood before. That is, until January 1996, when our daughter was married at home. A marquee in the garden was draped with silks and floral wreaths woven by a large number of enthusiastic volunteers, with flowers collected from around the community. Table settings were completed with baby pears from our garden, sprayed golden and, when they ran out, baby apples. It looked magnificent—a wedding at home in our garden!

Once we had gone through the usual mid-summer weather dramas, we still had to suffer a week of rain before the day. In the end, the marquee was erected early to allow the grass to dry out and the lawn was mown under canvas before the furniture was moved in. Trenches were dug around the tent edges to help divert water away from the marquee. Gardens were tidied, flowers organised, clothes ordered, hairdos planned.

And then there was the food . . . well, that had to be perfect. We'd asked Anne, a very talented local chef, to prepare the food for the celebration. Most of the recipes she used came from a book I had purchased at Rudyard Kipling's garden in Sussex, UK, a few years earlier. It was called *Recipes for a Perfect Country Weekend* by Sally Anne Scott, photography by Linda Burgess. I don't remember the gardens particularly but what I remember is buying the cookbook, which I have used to produce some wonderful menus over the years since.

However, the restricted space in my tiny kitchen and the steepish paths from the house to the marquee presented a challenge for Anne and her helpers. Of all the amazing and beautiful sights that day, one lasting memory is, of course, to do with the food and the sweet food in particular—we had lavender ice cream with gooey meringues and a chocolate wedding cake. There was no dried fruit in sight—a must for a daughter who could never stand raisins in a cake!

The perfection of the day and seeing a beautiful daughter married is forever linked to the subtle flavours of a true lavender ice cream. I remember saying to the newlyweds at the end of the day, 'I can't repeat this performance, you'd better stay married!'

Lavender and honey ice cream

This requires flowers from French lavender, and I like to use clover honey.

625ml cream
25ml milk
2/3 cup mild honey
6 large fresh lavender flower heads
2 eggs
pinch of salt

1 Put the cream, milk, honey and lavender in a heavy-based saucepan and bring it just to the boil, stirring occasionally, over a moderate heat.
2 Remove the pan from the heat and leave to cool for about 30 minutes to allow the lavender flavour to infuse.
3 Pour the cream mixture through a fine sieve and discard the lavender, then return the mixture to a cleaned saucepan and heat but do not boil.
4 Whisk together the eggs and salt in a separate bowl, then slowly add the hot cream mixture while continuing to whisk.
5 Cook over a low heat for about 5 minutes, stirring constantly with a wooden spoon, until the mixture thickens.
6 Pour the custard through a sieve into a clean bowl and cool completely, stirring occasionally.
7 Pour into an airtight freezer-proof container and put in the freezer. It will take at least 3 hours to set.

SERVES 8–10

Gooey meringues

(Adapted from *Recipes for a Perfect Country Weekend,* by Sally Anne Scott and Linda Burgess.)

285g caster sugar
5 egg whites
1 level tspn cornflour
1 tspn white vinegar
675g greengages (or yellow plums), stoned
150ml water
1 tspn maple syrup

1 Preheat the oven to 155°C. Line a baking tray with lightly oiled grease-proof paper or foil.
2 Beat half the sugar with the egg whites and continue to beat at maximum speed until very stiff.
3 Mix the cornflour with the remaining sugar and add to the first mixture, pulsing slowly if using a food processor or otherwise beat with an electric beater or mixer.
4 Mix in the vinegar.
5 Turn the oven down to 120°C.
6 Place teaspoonfuls of the mixture onto the prepared baking tray.
7 Bake for 1 hour or until the meringues have dried out and slide off the tray.

8 Turn off the oven, leaving the meringues inside for a further 30 minutes.

9 Remove from the oven.

10 The meringues should be hard on the outside but the inside will have the consistency of marshmallow.

11 Place the destoned fruit in a pan and add the water and maple syrup.

12 Bring quickly to the boil and boil until reduced by half.

13 Remove from the heat and leave to cool.

14 Serve the meringues with the fruit and whipped cream.

MAKES 20 LARGE OR 40 SMALL MERINGUES

'No raisin' chocolate mousse wedding cake

While we have lost the original, this recipe is very close in flavour and texture. You can adapt it for a wedding or other large event by multiplying the quantities and using a bigger cake tin.

For the cake
2½ cups ground almonds
2 cups icing sugar
½ cup plain flour
½ cup Dutch cocoa
1 tspn baking powder
5 eggs, beaten
250g butter, melted

For layering

500g good-quality dark chocolate (I like to use 70% cocoa butter)
2 cups cream
1 tsp vanilla

1 Preheat the oven to 160°C. Grease and line a 23cm springform tin.
2 Put the ground almonds, icing sugar, flour, cocoa and baking powder in a bowl and stir well.
3 Add the eggs and butter and gently mix until well combined.
4 Spoon into the prepared tin and bake for 1 hour until cooked when tested with a skewer.
5 Stand for 5 minutes, then transfer to a wire rack to cool.
6 Line a 20cm springform tin with cling film. Trim the top of the cake until it's flat. Slice the cake in half so you have two thin round cakes.
7 Take the cake pan and place on top of each cake, then trim the cakes so they fit into the tin.
8 Place one of the thin cakes into the cake pan.
9 For layering, melt all the chocolate in a heatproof bowl over a saucepan of simmering water. Stir until smooth.
10 In another bowl, beat the cream with the vanilla until it forms soft peaks, then fold this into the chocolate mixture.
11 Spoon half of the creamy chocolate mixture onto the cake in the tin then place the other half of the cake on top.
12 Spoon the remaining creamy chocolate mixture onto the cake and spread evenly.
13 Cover the cake and refrigerate overnight.
14 Next day, remove the cake from the mould and transfer to a serving plate or cake stand.
15 Finally, dust with extra cocoa and serve with fresh berry fruit of your choice.

SERVES 6–8

Food, family, friends and special events, they all merge at times. Conviviality around a table loaded with good food is a wonderful thing. When all the work of preparation is over and you take the first mouthful and it tastes good, you know you can relax. Then, on with the talking and sharing or even the debating and disagreeing—the food is there to centre you all, so that you can connect in new ways. Of course, there will be moments when the loudness and passion of debate can detract so much from the food that a halt must be called so due reverence can be delivered to the cook's creations!

The hope is that the art of conversation at a family meal will always be retained, however brief or simple the meal, and we continue to demarcate life with celebrations wherever and however we live, by getting around a table to talk and eat.

CHAPTER 17

Grandchildren arrive

The end of the 1990s heralded the beginning of a new generation and grandparenting for us along with the first of many visits to the small Australian town of Maitland in the lower Hunter Valley, where our daughter and son-in-law had settled. We delighted in a beautiful new granddaughter. Quite fortuitously, our son-in-law's employer, a coal company owner, is a connoisseur of the region's best offerings of food and wine. He was the surest of guides. The beginning of grandparenting in Australia and a new friendship in celebration of family, food, wine and the good things in life.

Little people came into our lives, once again. We are amazed by how much joy they bring along with a new perspective to family dining, as their appreciation of food, its variety and quality, develops by what is offered to them from an early age. Some were easier to feed than others, despite the same exposure to different foods. The biggest obstacle from one was a firm 'I don't like it,' a blanket statement made without actually trying the food in dispute.

The grandchildren have reinspired my everyday cooking, as they show their appreciation of food at Granny's. Favourite meals for them now, and sometimes their friends, include lamb rack done various ways, with a herb coating or with a breadcrumb crust helping to retain the moistness of the meat, and a potato cream dish.

In-a-hurry rack of lamb

Rack of lamb is great at any time.

1 rack of lamb
garlic
salt and pepper to taste (I use Maldon sea salt)
½ cup chopped rosemary
cooking oil

1 Preheat the oven to 250°C.
2 Trim off any excess fat from the rack.
3 Sear quickly on both sides in a hot heavy-based pan.
4 Rub all over with garlic, salt, pepper and chopped rosemary.
5 Pour some oil over and place in a baking tin.
6 Roast for 10 to 15 minutes.
7 Remove the tray from the oven and cover with tinfoil for a few minutes to allow last-minute cooking to take place outside the oven. Serve with grape jelly (see page 206).

SERVES 2

Lamb rack with herb crust

This recipe adds something special and the meat is super tender, having been baked inside the crust. It will impress friends, but takes a little longer to prepare. However, you can prepare these ahead of time, cover the crusted racks with plastic wrap and store in the fridge until required.

2 × 6 cutlet lamb racks
1 tbspn oil
salt and pepper
1 cup fresh breadcrumbs
3 cloves garlic
2 tbspn chopped parsley
2 tspn thyme
½ tspn finely grated lemon zest
60g butter, softened

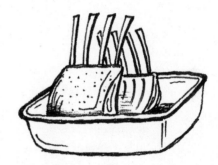

1 Preheat the oven to 250°C.
2 Rub the rack with a little oil and season with salt and pepper.
3 Heat the remaining oil in a frying pan over a high heat. Add the lamb and brown for 4 or 5 minutes. Remove and set aside, reserving the pan for later.
4 In a large bowl, mix the breadcrumbs, garlic, parsley, thyme and lemon zest.
5 Season, then mix in the butter to make a firm paste.
6 Firmly press a layer of breadcrumb mixture over the fat on the racks, leaving the bones and base clean.
7 If you wish, place tinfoil over the ends of the bones to prevent them from burning.
8 When you're just about ready to eat, bake in a baking dish for 12 to 15 minutes for medium-rare, or until cooked to your liking. Allow to rest.

SERVES 6

Papas a la crema

This is an absolute favourite with all ages, and it's always requested by our grand-daughter from Argentina. 'I want the papas a la crema por favor.'

4–6 large red or golden-skinned potatoes
600ml cream
100g butter
salt and pepper
fresh rosemary

1 Peel the potatoes and place in a bowl of cold water to prevent discoloration. Choose an earthenware or porcelain baking dish. I usually use an oval porcelain one for this family favourite.
2 Slice the potatoes into rounds and place across the dish in layers, until the dish is full.
3 Pour over the cream.
4 Cut the butter into knobs and place on the potato.
5 Season the dish and add fresh rosemary, chopped a little to release the flavour.
6 Bake in a medium oven for about 1 hour.

SERVES 6

Our grandchildren continue to increase their connection to us between watching and being involved with vegetable- and fruit-growing in the gardens and preparation of food for the table.

Growing and digging potatoes has become a favourite for some of them. I take immense pleasure from seeing the young ones biting into a perfect new potato boiled and dripping with butter and hearing their exclamation that it tastes delicious. It reminds me of time spent with my grandparents and brings back a flood of food memories from my grandmother's kitchen.

Blackcurrant and gooseberry picking is another activity they are keen to be involved in with their grandfather. Then, as always, there's the excitement of helping to make pastry and prepare the fruit for tarts to be eaten that night.

Blackcurrant and gooseberry tart

Blackcurrants and gooseberries both cook very quickly. Prepare the fruit by washing and, in the case of the gooseberries, topping and tailing them.

1 batch Sweet short pastry (see page 55)
3 cups cleaned fruit
sugar to taste (I allow 1 cup for a very tart tart)

1 Preheat the oven to 200°C.
2 Roll out the pastry and line a 23cm tart tin.
3 Put the fruit and sugar into a saucepan. Add just enough water to cover the bottom of the pan.
4 Heat gently until the fruit softens and the sugar has dissolved.
5 Pour the fruit into the uncooked pastry case.
6 If you have extra pastry, make a lattice pattern on top of the fruit.

7 Bake in the oven until the pastry is cooked and the fruit has reduced and thickened.
8 Serve with whipped cream.

SERVES 6

I introduce all the grandchildren to jellies made with real fruit juice—blackcurrant, strawberry and rhubarb are particular favourites. It is immensely satisfying for me to see my grandchildren and their friends eating and enjoying home-made real fruit jellies.

Real fruit jelly

These delicious jellies are a great favourite with the grandchildren, especially when put into pretty moulds. I use blackcurrants, strawberries, apples, blackberries, plums, rhubarb or any of these in combination—it depends on the season and availability.

For strawberry and redcurrant jelly
250g fresh strawberries, hulled and chopped
250g fresh or frozen redcurrants
1 cup sugar
2–2½ leaves gelatine (depending on how firm you want the jelly)
water—enough to cover the fruit while cooking

1 Chop two or three strawberries into the serving bowl or individual dishes you will be using for the jelly.

2 Put the remainder of the strawberries and redcurrants in a saucepan with enough water to cover and simmer for a few minues until the fruit has softened.
3 Strain the cooked fruit through a sieve or jelly bag and measure the liquid.
4 Take 400mls of the liquid (if you have more you can freeze it for future use).
5 Pour the liquid back into the saucepan, add the sugar and heat until sugar is dissolved.

Spanish cream with strawberry jelly

This attractive and lovely dessert which came from my mother and grandmother was much loved by my youngest son. It has been brought up to date by the addition of the real strawberry jelly. Although it's a bit fiddly to make over two days as each layer sets, it's easy to serve. It looks pretty in a glass bowl or individual glasses and is a great hit with all ages.

3½ leaves gelatine
600ml milk
3 eggs, separated
3 tbspn sugar
1 tspn vanilla essence
1 batch Real fruit jelly (made with strawberries, see page 130)
1 punnet fresh strawberries

1 Place the serving bowl or dishes into the fridge to chill.
2 Soak the gelatine in water until soft.

3 Heat the milk until it comes to a simmer, stirring all the time.

4 Beat the egg yolks and sugar together until pale. Add the squeezed out gelatine to the milk and stir until it dissolves. Add the egg and sugar mixture to the milk and gelatine.

5 Continue stirring over the heat until the egg and milk mixture thickens, then remove from the heat to cool.

6 Beat the egg whites until stiff and beat in the vanilla. Fold into the custard mixture.

7 Pour into chilled dishes, cover and put in the fridge until required.

8 Separately, some hours later or even the next day, prepare a Real fruit jelly using 500g fresh strawberries (see page 132). Set the jelly aside to cool.

9 Meanwhile, rinse the punnet of strawberries, then hull the berries and cut into halves.

10 Arrange the strawberries cut-side down to cover the top of the Spanish cream.

11 Carefully pour the cooled jelly mixture onto the strawberries and put back in the fridge to set.

12 Serve chilled.

SERVES 6

I have never understood the theory of making separate children's meals for younger members of the family. My grandchildren, who spent each summer with family in Argentina, were exposed to adult food tastes from an early age, in fact from a few months old. I remember seeing during a visit to the family in Argentina the babies of the family given a piece of the roasted meat held by the parent to suck the juices from, as we all sat around the family table. In the 70s and 80s we were proud to introduce new flavours and taste experiences to our children, but we still prepared separate baby food or children's food platters when they were very young. Our Argentine grandchildren ate whatever the family was having, experiencing a range of tastes and participating in the full eating experience. Their expectations around food, for quality of taste and texture, were heightened from an early age. Our Australian grandchildren, despite having early food experiences more akin to those experienced by my own children and exposure to the gorgeous fresh food of the Hunter Valley and later when they shifted to Townsville, in Northern Queensland, have had very different responses to food even after the best efforts of their mother and grandmother. Not all have responded positively to their exposure to good food tastes! One out of the three has continued to have a passionate interest and adventure with tastes and as a teenager this shows in her own cooking interests and abilities. I like to hope that the more positive experiences that young children have with different flavours, the more interested and adventurous they will become.

CHAPTER 18

Forestry tour and a long lunch

It was September 2000 and we were halfway through a tour—the only organised tour I have been involved in before or since, as I prefer to do my own thing when I travel. I was accompanying my husband, who had planned and was leading a Forest and Garden Tour for thirteen keen Kiwis. By this point we had already visited South America, Scotland, Wales and England, the latter being immersed in a very disruptive petrol strike. But here we were, heading south to France and the city of Toulouse.

I felt the lovely hot blast of warm air as we disembarked from the flight. The Pyrenees were so clear in the background. Our driver, Marcel, and Amélie, our guide and interpreter, were there to meet us. We journeyed directly to Carcassonne, the famous fortified town northeast of Toulouse, where we stayed the night. The next morning we were met by forestry representatives from the district. For this day, our first in France, the itinerary listed 'Forest tour, with lunch to follow'.

It was an exquisite morning with hot sunshine as we drove to meet our hosts at the base of Montagne Noire, north of Carcassonne. There were forests in all directions. After the official welcome we left to explore, transported in a mixture of cars and a bus. It was a fantastic journey through exquisite forests, some areas so perfect they appeared to be man-made, yet we were assured they were natural. Magic indeed for tree lovers, but added to these outdoor pleasures was the luncheon—not the boxed sandwiches and fruit you might expect on a forest tour in New Zealand or the United States. No, this was to be a long lunch in a restaurant. Tucked away in this sparsely populated, largely forested area of France was a gastronomique feast waiting in Aux Epis, a restaurant near the small village of Anglès, near Mazamet.

Amongst the passionate talk of the French forestier and rapid translations across the table, we were introduced to the pleasures of the long lunch, a truly memorable five-course feast. It began with a terrine de lapin (rabbit terrine). This was followed by a salad with bacon and nuts, a version of which I have included below.

Salade aux lardons et noix

1 large buttercrunch lettuce
4 tspn olive oil
25ml walnut oil
25ml red wine vinegar
1 tspn Dijon mustard
salt and pepper
70g freshly cracked walnuts, broken into pieces
150g bacon slices, cut into small pieces
4 slices of baguette, cut into bite-sized cubes
1 clove garlic, cut in half

1 Arrange the lettuce leaves in a bowl.

2 Mix together the olive oil, walnut oil, vinegar, mustard, salt and pepper.

3 Blanche the walnuts with boiling water for 1 minute, drain, and pat dry.

4 Cook the bacon until crisp, then remove from the pan to a paper towel to drain.

5 Add the walnuts to the pan and cook for a few minutes, until browned. Remove to a paper towel to drain.

6 Fry the baguette pieces into cubes in the last of the oil remaining in the pan to make croutons.

7 Add all the ingredients to the lettuce in the bowl and toss well.

SERVES 4

Then we were served our main course—poulet confit avec haricots verts et pommes de terre. It sounds a lot better than chicken with French beans and potatoes, but there's nothing nicer than simple food prepared with care. Fortunately, the servings were not too large, so we could savour each course. Next the cheese plate—Roquefort with a little pot of crème fraîche with honey and sultanas on the side and, lastly, the dessert. What better for dessert than a perfect tarte Tatin?

Tarte Tatin

It took me 20 years to realise a great tarte Tatin is much easier to produce with the right dish. The purchase of a Tatin cooking pan (made in France but bought in New Zealand because it was so heavy to carry) made all the difference. Now, I can serve this wonderful dessert without fuss. I sometimes use quinces in season instead of the traditional apples, and it's best served barely warm.

For the pastry
225g flour
1 tbspn caster sugar plus extra to sprinkle
1 small pinch of salt
150g soft unsalted butter
2 tbspn crème fraîche, sour cream or mascarpone
1 tbspn cream

For the filling
120g soft unsalted butter
150g caster sugar
900g crisp eating apples (Cox's orange, Braeburn or Scarlett)

1 To make the pastry, sift the flour into a bowl, add the sugar and salt and stir to combine.
2 Cut the butter into small pieces, then work it into the flour with your fingertips.
3 Once the butter has been absorbed, work in the crème fraîche and the cream.
4 Roll into a ball, wrap in plastic wrap and chill for at least half an hour.
5 Meanwhile, make the filling by melting half the butter in a 30cm Tatin dish. Remove from the heat.
6 Sprinkle half the sugar over the melted butter and swirl to mix, making sure the edge of the dish is well coated.
7 Peel, core and cut the apples into pieces. Either cut them in half, which is traditional, or into chunky quarters, which I prefer.

8 Arrange the apples over the melted butter and sugar, packing them in tightly.

9 Sprinkle them with the rest of the sugar and dot with the rest of the butter.

10 Preheat the oven to 220°C.

11 Place the pan with the apples on top of the stove over a moderately high heat for 10 to 15 minutes until the butter and sugar look golden and lightly caramelised. You will need to keep a sharp eye on it to make sure the mixture does not turn too brown.

12 Remove the pan from the heat and leave until just cool enough to handle.

13 Meanwhile, lightly dust a rolling pin with flour and roll out the pastry, not too thinly. Make sure your circle of pastry is 5cm larger than the pan. You may need to use your hands as well as the pastry tends to crumble.

14 Place the rolled out pastry over the apples. Using your fingers, tuck it in well between the apples and the edge of the tin.

15 Sprinkle a little sugar over the surface to make it crunchy and prick in several places with a fork.

16 Bake for about 30 minutes, until the pastry is golden.

17 Remove from the oven and leave to cool for a few minutes.

18 Cover with a serving dish larger than the Tatin dish.

19 Turn over and unmould onto the serving dish, knocking the serving dish against the work surface and tapping the tin sharply. Your perfect Tatin should fall onto the serving dish.

20 Rearrange the apples a little if necessary.

SERVES 6–8

CHAPTER 19

A new millennium

The following year we returned for late summer in the northern hemisphere. Schools were back, the worst effects of tourism over for another season and the weather had pretty much settled into gorgeous hot days with even temperatures. In southern France and Italy the evenings were still warm enough to be outside.

We had been travelling for the earlier part of September—me with my husband on business in the US and the friends we were meeting had been travelling for pleasure in Italy. They found the villa and rented the car and we had directions to find them. Our flight delivered us to Rome and the next day we caught a train north into Umbria. Our friends Sarah and Philip would pick us up at the nearest train station for a short drive to the villa in Montefalco. We were excited to meet up at last—there were hugs and kisses, bags stowed in the car and many stories to tell. We were all full of new experiences after a few weeks of separate travel, in sharply contrasting environments.

The most notable of these had been a cheese-eating incident involving our friends. 'You can't believe what her lips looked like,' her partner told us. 'Her whole face was swollen and she couldn't breathe. I thought I was going to have to perform a tracheotomy with a knife from the café. We were saved by one of the waitresses, who drove us at speed down country roads to the hospital. I travelled in the car behind. I wasn't allowed to see her at first, until they got the allergic reaction under control.' Ever since our friend has had to exercise caution with Italian goat's milk cheese and products made with them. Death by cheese in Umbria is not an attractive thought.

So here we were on 10 September 2001, enjoying the languid late summer in the Umbrian countryside. It had been a long, hot summer full of tourists for the locals and there was a feeling in the air: 'They've done us over a bit, but we're still here. Things will settle back soon.'

Our villa wasn't what I'd imagined—it was quite modern, but the building itself was charming and everything was clean and cool. Shutters opened to reveal rolling valleys and acres of olive trees . . . the pace was slow . . . the swimming pool was refreshing and we were friends together about to begin a new adventure.

The next day we began our exploration of the locality—we did the usual touristy things and had a wonderful picnic on a wild hillside and in the early evening we went in search of dinner. The village of Montefalco had cobbled streets and limited vehicle access. We had to walk into the centre of the village and there it was, Il Coccorone, the restaurant we had heard so much about. There was a delicious aroma inviting us in. Meat was cooking in an open-fire oven, a little fan on the hearth spreading the fire's heat evenly. One side of the restaurant was for more formal dining, and on the other was an open café with a large TV screen above the bar. We sat and made our order but began to notice the TV was very loud. One of our party walked over to the barman to ask if he would turn it down. The other diners had stopped eating and were absorbed. It seemed peculiar. I tried to look at the screen, but it was difficult. Why were they so distracted? The meal was delicious, veal with grapes for two and pheasant for two, followed by a perfect panna cotta.

The perfect panna cotta

I like to make this in pretty glasses but you can also set panna cotta in a mould or moulds to tip out just before serving.

3 leaves gelatine
1 vanilla pod
600ml cream
150ml milk
150g sugar

1 Soak the gelatine in cold water until soft.
2 Split the vanilla pod and scoop the seeds into a saucepan. Add the cream, milk and sugar and place the pan over a low heat.
3 Heat to simmering, and when the sugar has dissolved remove from the heat.
4 Squeeze excess water out of the gelatine and add to the warm milky mixture. Stir until the gelatine has fully dissolved.
5 Pour the liquid into 6 serving glasses. Cover with plastic wrap and put in the fridge to set.

SERVES 6

As we completed our meal, the waiter began to talk in an animated way to Mark. He mentioned, uno, due, tre . . . quattro. He added to his verbal description with a physical rendition of an aeroplane, arms outstretched, and began to circle and with gesticulations, both physical and vocal, he acted out an explosion. Those images of aeroplanes flying down and crashing were obviously more significant than a fiction movie. It suddenly occurred to us something very unusual was happening somewhere in the world. We listened, straining to understand, and quickly realised New York was the location and the planes, on closer inspection, were commercial airliners. Each of us reacted differently as the understanding of the enormity of what had happened dawned. We were terribly distressed, but at least we had each other to share our distress with—the worst thing about the following hours was not being able to understand the fast Italian overlay on CNN.

It was an event none of us could ever have imagined and it was far worse than anything from a horror movie. Was it real? We asked if there was another TV in the village. This restaurant felt too public, too difficult for us to get close to listen. The proprietor took us downstairs to another TV he thought may have an English CNN channel, but it didn't work. We left the restaurant and made our way up the street to a small bar crowded with locals. There was a TV in the corner and people were glued to it except two young men who were just beside the TV, absolutely immersed in their PlayStation game. I looked over the shoulder of one and saw to my amazement they were playing a shooting game, putting all their efforts into exploding as many things as they could. Too busy to notice the dreadful reality to their right that was so desperate, scary and world changing. What began as a wonderful rural eating experience ended in this crazy scene.

By now we were piecing together what had happened. The last thing we saw that night was bombing in Afghanistan. We knew we were at a momentous place in history but we were unable to make contact with the rest of the world to find out more—all telephone lines were blocked. It was two days before we could get some more information in our hotel in Rome and another three days before we got hold of an English-language newspaper and by then we were in Copenhagen.

Our flight from Rome to Singapore was diverted to Copenhagen, where we had an unscheduled stop-over for twelve hours—world-wide airline timetables were in post-9/11 tatters. Eventually, we made it to Rome, where we were staying near the main railway station. We left our hotel late one evening to make our way towards Ristorante La Cisterna—built in 1632, it's the oldest restaurant in Rome. In the eighteenth century, the neighbourhood was raised to prevent flooding from the River Tiber. Over the years, many important people have dined at La Cisterna—from Picasso to Miro, King Farouk, Princess Grace of Monaco, Walt Disney and Rita Hayworth—but I was more interested in the promise of delicious food and La Cisterna's reputation as a fascinating and unique restaurant. It proved to be all of that.

We thought we would save on a taxi fare and go by bus—we caught the 175 bus in what we thought would be good time. The journey dragged on and panic set in when we realised the bus was in an area we didn't recognise. It seemed to be on an enormous detour. It was already 9.20 pm and we realised we'd never make our reservation. When the two old men in front of us got off, so did we too. Fortunately, a couple in the only lit area of an otherwise darkened street were very helpful. They rang a cab for us, which delivered us in a few minutes and we were certainly ready for dinner and, to our surprise, we were on time after all!

We weren't disappointed. At first glimpse La Cisterna was eccentric and slightly decrepit, but full of fresh flowers, starched white tablecloths, happy diners and waiters who behaved more like 'mad' actors. The food was absolutely delicious—fettuccine alla papalina, pollo arrosto o alla nerone and abbacchio al torno con patate, and we finished with a dessert to die for, zabaglione (see recipe on page 98).

However, the real highlight came after the meal when all but one other table of diners had left. We were gathered up by these people and taken downstairs to the cave. It is the last remaining piece of the original underground restaurant. Here we were offered champagne and introduced to our fellow diners, who turned out to be members of Passiflora Society International. La Cisterna had lived up to its promise, delivering a unique and memorable food experience with the bonus of contact details for joining the international society for the preservation and development of passionflowers! While I couldn't get recipes from La Cisterna, I have enjoyed experimenting and trying to recreate their dishes in my everyday cooking.

Pollo arrosto alla limone

1 small free-range chicken
salt and freshly ground pepper
1 whole lemon
fresh rosemary, roughly chopped
extra virgin olive oil
½ cup dry white wine

1 Preheat the oven to 160°C.
2 Season the inside of the chicken with salt and pepper.
3 Place the lemon inside the chicken cavity. Rub the outside of the chicken all over with salt and rosemary.
4 Place the chicken in a skillet with oil and quickly brown on all sides.
5 Transfer to the oven and roast for 1½ hours.
6 To serve, place the chicken on a serving dish.
7 Pour the wine into the skillet and heat for a few moments, scraping up all the browned bits, and serve this as a sauce with the chicken.

SERVES 6

Braciole alla pizzaiola

Pizzaiola refers to the thin slices of beef used in this great everyday dish.

60ml extra virgin olive oil
1 garlic clove, peeled
4-6 thin slices beef (I use schnitzel)
400g tomatoes, peeled and coarsely chopped (or 1 × 400g can chopped tomato)
salt and freshly ground pepper
1 tbspn chopped fresh oregano or 2 tspn dried oregano
4 potatoes, peeled and sliced

1 Preheat the oven to 180°C.
2 Heat the oil and garlic in a pan over high heat.
3 Add the meat and brown on both sides.
4 Add the tomatoes, season with salt and pepper and bring to the boil, then reduce the heat.
5 Sprinkle the oregano over the meat and tomatoes, partially cover the pan and simmer for 5 more minutes to reduce the sauce.
6 Transfer to an ovenproof dish and place the potatoes on top of the meat and sauce and season with salt and pepper.
7 Cover the dish with a lid or foil and bake for 20 to 30 minutes, but make sure it doesn't dry out.

SERVES 6

Chorizo, fennel and rosemary rigatoni

This pasta dish is a firm family favourite.

1 small onion
3 cloves garlic
1 fennel bulb
3 sprigs fresh rosemary
extra virgin olive oil
1 tspn smoked paprika
½ cup chardonnay
400g tomato passata or purée
1 large or 2 small chorizo
500g rigatoni No. 24
½ cup cream
½ cup grana padano or parmigiano-reggiano
12 green olives, chopped
chopped parsley

1 Finely chop the onion, garlic, fennel and rosemary.
2 Heat a heavy-bottomed saucepan, splash in some olive oil then sauté the chopped ingredients for about 30 seconds.
3 Add the paprika and stir in the wine, then cook for 1 minute to reduce the liquid.
4 Add the tomato passata or purée, reduce the heat and simmer for 10 minutes.
5 Slice the chorizo into small pieces. Sear it quickly in another pan and then add to the tomato sauce. Mix it in and place to one side.
6 Cook the pasta in a big saucepan of boiling, salted water until al dente.
7 Once cooked, drizzle over some olive oil to prevent it sticking together.

8 Mix the cream into the pasta sauce and heat through.

9 Check the seasoning and adjust, if required. (It might need salt.) Stir the sauce through the cooked pasta and leave on the heat for a couple of minutes to warm through.

10 Place into four bowls, and grate the cheese over the top.

11 Sprinkle with chopped olives and parsley, then add an extra drizzle of olive oil.

12 Finish with a good grind of black pepper.

SERVES 4

CHAPTER 20

Fish and forest

Two memorable and delicious food experiences arose from our business connections in the United States. Both involved boats, water and forests—the first was on the west coast in beautiful Puget Sound and Olympic Peninsula, and the other was on the east coast, on Mount Desert Island, which is the largest island off the Maine coast. Good food and wine and conviviality around a table so often provided us with an entrée to many business ventures, resulting in both commercial commitments and valued friendships. I first learnt about cedar-planked salmon in Washington State. A specialty of our hosts, we enjoyed this delicious method of cooking salmon on a number of occasions, most memorably cruising in Puget Sound and again out on a deck overlooking the beautiful Olympic Peninsula under a nearly full moon with volcanic Mount Rainier in the background.

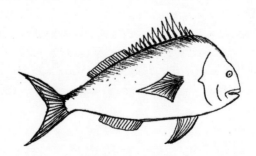

Cedar-planked salmon

In this recipe the salmon cooks in its own juices, making it deliciously moist. You'll need an untreated cedar plank approximately 40 × 12 centimetres.

2 × 500g salmon fillets, deboned and skinned
salt and pepper
6 tspn Dijon mustard
6 tspn brown sugar

1 Soak the cedar plank in salted water for two hours. Drain.
2 Generously season the salmon with salt and pepper.
3 Lay the fillets on the plank and carefully spread the mustard on top and sides of the salmon.
4 Sprinkle the brown sugar on the mustard.
5 Preheat the oven to grill at 190°C or bake at 180°C.
6 Grill for 12 to 20 minutes or bake for 10 minutes, depending on the thickness of the fillets.

SERVES 4–6

On Mount Desert Island, near the township of Bar Harbour, we had a fabulous lobster bake. The lobsters, dark brown when brought in from the sea, turn the most wonderful bright red when cooked. Our host had a cooker set up on the deck of his house. We sat and ate under the full moon, seen this time from the opposite coast, enjoying stories from some of the locals. It was a great introduction to a new business relationship, one that involved growing sustainable forests.

The following morning we breakfasted on fresh raspberries, blueberries and melon, sitting on the deck looking out to the bay and beyond. Then, once again, we headed to Europe. It had seemed easy when we set the itinerary weeks before in faraway New Zealand. Scheduling two business dinners back to back in Europe, one in eastern France and the other in northwest Germany, seemed feasible. As always, with Mark, schedules were tight and we thought no more about it. Despite getting lost, we arrived in Béligneux, near Lyons, in good time. There our first hosts had their main home and business administration centre. It was a delight to reconnect with Jean-Claude and Sylvie—this time on their territory. She was a great cook and we enjoyed the warmth and elegance of their home, where we were treated to a beautiful, simple and delicious home-cooked meal. Here, I was introduced to the dessert île flottante (floating island), also known as oeufs à la neige (eggs in the snow).

For me, that perfect dessert cemented our friendship, one which has carried on through the years despite distance and language difficulties. Sylvie's wonderful ability to produce simple delicious fresh meals for her family and friends has always impressed me.

Later, Sylvie and Jean-Claude hosted us at their summer residence in Vallauris, on the Côte d'Azur, near Cannes. When we were in Vallauris, I watched Sylvie's organisational skills with interest, noting the menus she chose when we were with her family, which was always extended and always included her grandchildren. I've learnt many many useful tips from her for stress-free meal preparation that have helped me with my large family over the summers that have followed. For example, freezing crêpes ready for the grandchildren's breakfast and how to make perfect mayonnaise.

Sylvie's mayonnaise

Sylvie always whisks her mayonnaise by hand, but you can use an electric beater or food processor. Try to have your ingredients at room temperature and warm a 1–1.2 litre mixing bowl before you start. Remember to add the oil slowly at first, drop by drop. Once the mixture has started to emulsify or thicken, you can add the remaining oil more quickly. And, as reminded by Julia Child (and I have no idea why), if you're going to use the electric beater you must use the whole egg rather than just the yolks.

3 egg yolks
275–400ml olive oil or salad oil (or a mixture of the two)
1 tbspn wine vinegar or lemon juice
½ tspn salt
¼ tspn dried or prepared mustard (I like to use Dijon mustard)
2 tbspn boiling water

1 Beat the egg yolks until thick and creamy.
2 Make sure the oil is tepid and start adding, drop by drop, continuing to whisk until the sauce is very thick.
3 Add the vinegar or lemon juice, salt and mustard and continue whisking until all the remaining oil has been blended in. If the sauce becomes too thick, add an extra drop or two of vinegar or lemon juice.
4 Lastly, beat in the boiling water and season to taste with extra vinegar, lemon juice, salt, pepper or mustard, as required.

In this part of France, small pieces of a savoury loaf are served as an aperitif. We saw them everywhere, including pre-packaged at petrol stations. We made the terrible mistake one day of buying some when filling the car—they looked home-made, but the first bite confirmed that was not the case. We hastily got rid of them, not wanting to taint our memory of the real thing introduced to us by Sylvie.

Savoury loaf aperitif

Slices of this tasty loaf are perfect to serve with early evening drinks.

3 eggs
200g plain flour
1 tspn baking powder
1½ cups grated emmental cheese
1 cup diced ham
1 cup pitted green or black olives
1 tbspn fresh herbs (thyme, marjoram)
200ml milk, approximately (enough to make a batter)

1 Heat the oven to 175°C. Grease two small loaf tins or one large loaf tin.
2 Beat the eggs in a large bowl.
3 Add all the other dry ingredients then, mixing gently, add the milk.
4 Divide the mixture into the prepared tins and bake for 45 minutes or until cooked.
5 Remove from the oven and wait until cool before turning out of the tins and slicing. Cut into small bite-sized pieces for serving. Best served cold, especially in hot climates.

The original plan had been to meet Jean-Claude, look at his forests and factories, then enjoy dinner and an overnight stay in his home. Leaving our car in Lyons, we would travel by train to Düsseldorf the next day. Jean-Claude, however, wanted Mark to see some forests far away in the interior. 'But what about the connection in Germany?' No worries, he said, he'd organised a helicopter.

He reassured us the other colleague could be called and our dinner and overnight stay transferred to the next day. I'd met the couple from Germany on a forestry tour in New Zealand and knew how this would throw them. How could their hugely busy schedule be rearranged and how would she, so super-organised, feel about the re-arrangement? Somehow, the Frenchman placated the German and our schedule was rewritten. Now, I was flying to Düsseldorf alone to be met by a chauffeur-driven car and taken to our German business hosts' home in Krefeld. Mark was coming later, and in the meantime I was to act as if there was nothing untoward about arriving for a forestry business meeting without the forestry businessman in tow—he would still be flying around central France!

After the helicopter flight, Mark was going to make a quick trip on a later flight to meet us at a restaurant in Krefeld that had already been booked. I had calculated that, even if everything went according to Jean-Claude's plan, Mark was going to be very, very late for dinner! I was trying to calm my rising panic as to how I would explain Mark's lateness and this time I had been complicit, so it wasn't going to be easy.

Three of us, our Geman host and hostess and I, arrived at Companina, a beautiful little restaurant, at eight o'clock sharp despite my every attempt to delay our departure from their beautiful home. But, with German precision, the car was ready in good time and we left for the restaurant exactly on schedule. An hour and a half later there was still no sign of Mark. How was I going to keep the conversation going and allay our hosts' fears? It was no mean feat, and that meal in Krefeld remains etched in my memory for not just the food but the feeling of unease as we munched our way through the entire evening without the forestry businessman.

A starter came out and went—tiny breads looking like pillows, with the finest butter and salami. An entrée came out and went—rare tuna of fantastic quality in a delicious sauce. Then the main came out and went—turkey with chanterelles accompanied by a German potato dish.

Still no sign of Mark! 'Perhaps he has missed his flight?' My hosts asked if they should ring the airport.

'Should they call Jean-Claude?' I assured them we'd hear from Mark if there was a problem. He knew the telephone number of the restaurant. On the one hand, I was trying to show how concerned I was about his lateness and on the other I was trying to conceal the knowledge we had known all along he would be very, very late. The food was delicious and the service impeccable at this little treasure of Italian brilliance tucked away in a northern corner of Germany.

Mark finally turned up, smartly dressed and beaming his placatory smile, at ten o'clock, by which time we had already eaten our dessert—perfect fresh white peaches peeled, sliced and sitting in a hot sweet sauce with ice cream on the side. His hair was a bit wild, but then he'd just made a mad dash from central France by helicopter, train, plane and car to board an Air France flight to Düsseldorf with just minutes to spare.

The chef very kindly created a dinner specially for Mark, including a dessert. Another wine was uncorked and the conversation flowed until after midnight and started up again from six in the morning over breakfast until our host departed at eight o'clock.

Three home-cooked meals, one in a restaurant, with two connections retained and two missed, and I had yet to make an île flottante!

Île flottante

For this delicate dessert of French origin, soft poached meringue islands float in a sea of crème anglaise (a light custard sauce).

450ml milk
150g sugar
1 vanilla bean, split lengthways
3 eggs, separated
1 tspn cornflour
pinch of salt
1 tspn orange flower water
extra milk for poaching the meringue

For the spun caramel
175g white sugar
3 tbspns cold water

1 Place the milk, half of the sugar and the vanilla bean in a saucepan and bring to the boil. Remove from the heat and take out the vanilla bean.
2 Beat the egg yolks with the cornflour in a bowl.
3 Pour the warm milk slowly into the egg mixture, stirring constantly with a wooden spoon.

4 Return to a low heat and stir until the custard thickens enough to coat the back of a spoon, making sure it does not boil or the eggs will curdle. Add the orange flower water.

5 Remove from the heat and pour the custard through a fine sieve into a large serving dish.

6 Whisk the egg whites with a pinch of salt until stiff. Add the remaining sugar and continue beating.

7 Heat a saucepan of milk to simmering and poach egg-sized spoonfuls of the meringue mixture for 1 minute. Turn them over gently and poach for another minute. Drain and place on top of the custard.

8 Just before serving make the caramel by placing the sugar and water in a heavy-based saucepan and simmering over a medium heat until the caramel turns golden. Don't stir, but shake the pan to prevent sticking.

9 Allow to cool slightly then spin the caramel in fine threads over the egg whites with a wooden spoon.

SERVES 6

Dark cherry clafoutis

Traditionally, clafoutis is made with cherries. This delicious dessert couldn't be simpler—pancake batter poured over fresh fruit and baked in the oven until golden.

If you are prepared to risk large dental bills in favour of added flavour you can leave the stones in the cherries, but give all the diners fair warning!

3 eggs
100g sugar
½ tspn vanilla

pinch of salt
1 tbspn Kirsch (or dark rum)
75g flour
375ml milk
20g butter, softened
500g cherries, washed and pitted
icing sugar for dusting

1 Preheat the oven to 200°C.
2 Beat the eggs and sugar until light and frothy.
3 Add the vanilla, salt and Kirsch.
4 Stir in the flour and fold the mixture over gently.
5 Add the milk and just mix through.
6 Rub a 20–24cm ovenproof dish with the soft butter and place in the cherries.
7 Pour the batter over and bake for 40-45 minutes.
8 If a skewer inserted into the centre comes out clean, the clafoutis is done.
9 Sprinkle with icing sugar and serve immediately.

SERVES 6

Quince clafoutis

This is a great alternative to cherry clafoutis when you have a lot of ripe quinces.

For the poached quinces

300ml white wine
250g caster sugar
2 quinces, peeled, quartered and cored
½ tspn whole cloves
1 tspn each black and white peppercorns
1 bay leaf
1 cinnamon quill
1 star anise
1 cup water

For the batter

2 eggs
1 egg yolk
55g caster sugar
pinch of salt
75g plain flour
250ml milk
sunflower oil

1 To poach the quinces, put all the ingredients in a flameproof casserole. Cover the surface with a round of baking paper, bring to a simmer, then cover with a lid and simmer over a low heat for 3 hours or bake in a low-heat oven until tender and deep pink.
2 To make the batter, whisk the eggs, egg yolk, caster sugar and salt together in a bowl until thick and pale. In four batches, whisk in the flour and milk. Strain the mixture through a fine sieve to remove any lumps then set aside for 30 minutes.
3 Preheat the oven to 200°C.
4 Brush four shallow 14cm ramekins with oil and place on two baking trays.
5 Place the trays in the oven for 10 minutes or until the dishes are hot.

6 Divide the quinces into the ramekins, reserving the quince syrup to drizzle over the cooked clafoutis.

7 Pour the batter over the quinces (they should be covered) and bake for 20 to 25 minutes, swapping the position of the trays after 10 minutes, until the clafoutis is golden and puffed. Serve immediately with a scoop of ice cream and drizzled with quince syrup.

SERVES 4

CHAPTER 21

Morocco bound

What I loved about Morocco were the surprises everywhere I looked. Going into the medina in Marrakech for the first time, I vividly remember carrying my bags along stone-tiled alleys too narrow for a vehicle that were dusty, dirty and crowded with pedestrians, bicycles and donkeys. The city wall was on one side and the walls of houses on the other, each home marked by huge wooden doors. We were impressed by the beautiful and intricate carvings on the doors, knowing that behind them the magic of everyday life in Marrakech was carrying on just as it had for centuries. As we made our way along the bustling alleys with their dust, flies, and the pungent smell of sweat and hot animals, a door would open and we would sneak a peek inside where all was calm and beautiful—the enormous contrast was completely unexpected.

We were staying in a riad—a traditional Morrocan house with a courtyard garden—and there, too, we found peace and beauty and a welcome escape from the hustle and bustle of the city. The food was stunning; dinner was served on the rooftop in the early evenings, overlooking the rooftops of the medina, and in the eastern distance the southern Atlas Mountains stood stark in their bare beauty. The tagine, with its long-handled spoon held so neatly in the hole in the lid of the dish, looked perfect. Floating curtains gently protected us from the late sun. Our waitress-cum-housemaid was gentle and quiet. Memories of those evenings include white-washed surfaces, cushions and carpets in rich warm colours and unique designs, and the tagines—lamb or chicken.

One day we took our host's suggestion to visit a nearby restaurant—we had been assured of a great dining experience. And so it was. After walking for what seemed like a long time up and down numerous alleys with our guide, we stood outside an enormous dark-stained wooden door and knocked. It was opened and we stepped inside. From the moment we entered there was a fairy-tale quality to the experience. Such beauty awaited us, and coolness and peace.

We were in a huge space and looking up we could see, as is often the way with these buildings in the medina, the centre had no roof. The blue sky was the ceiling to the central courtyard of the restaurant. It was two storeys high and from the balcony came the sound of Lisa Ekdahl's voice providing a relaxing musical ambience. A surprise to hear the dulcet tones of a Swedish jazz singer in this setting but perfect all the same. On the walls were all sorts of beautiful artwork—the space doubled as a gallery.

Diners sat around at tables in the courtyard and some in small alcoves around the edges. The food, as we experienced so often in Morocco, was delicate, full of exquisite tastes and textures and colour. There was always an astonishing variety of small tasting dishes—dates, oranges, couscous, olives, almonds, meats, spice. Rose petals were everywhere, on the tabletops, in the fountains and numerous water features. Never before had I been surrounded by as many rose petals as I was in Morocco, whether I was eating or sleeping!

We ate another tagine, and then sweet treats—delicately flavoured Turkish delight, lemon or rose. And then the tea ceremony at the end of a meal, the waiter resplendent in his uniform of harem-style pants, red jacket and hat, huge ornamental silver teapot in hand. The posture he adopted was almost balletic as he reached high in the air to pour fresh mint tea, which miraculously landed in our clear glass cups. I was enthralled each time this happened, but at this restaurant it was simply spectacular.

The next day our driver took us into the Atlas Mountains. This is Berber country. I have a husband who is determined to see mountain cedar growing in their native habitat, and I'm keen to meet some locals. We left early and after several hours of driving we walked for another few hours into the mountains. As we began the climb up the narrow stony pathways, I could smell something delicious. Perched on rocky outcrops, tagines sat on bowls of hot coals, quietly simmering their delicious contents. The cooks were close by, their houses tucked into the rocky mountain terrain. Mouth-watering smells, but not on offer to tourists. Despite walking for hours, we got nowhere near the distant cedars, which at every turn seemed further away, and we realised we needed to save them for another time. We left Morocco promising to return.

Next time, I want to experience the seafood of Essaouira on Morocco's Atlantic Coast. At home I enjoy making a chicken, lemon and olive dish for family and friends—it bears a resemblance to tagine cooking but can be made using any heavy earthenware or cast-iron dish with tinfoil to seal in the steam if the dish doesn't have have a lid.

Berber tagine

This can be made with chicken pieces or lamb. If using lamb, I buy a rolled lamb roast and unroll it, remove the skin and all visible fat and cut it into small pieces.

It can be simmered on the stove top or cooked in the oven at 180°C.

650g chicken or lamb
sea salt and freshly ground black pepper
3 tbspn olive oil
1 large onion, sliced
2 cloves garlic, chopped
1 tspn ground cinnamon
1 tspn ground ginger
1 tspn ground cumin
200g large juicy raisins or 12 large dried apricots
200g carrots, peeled and sliced
400g potatoes, peeled and thickly sliced
3 tbspn clear honey
2 cups chicken stock
½ cup black olives, for serving
¼ cup chopped fresh coriander or parsley, for serving

1 Season the chicken or lamb with the salt and pepper.
2 Heat a heavy-based frying pan and add a little of the oil.
3 Brown the chicken or lamb in batches for 1 to 2 minutes on each side.
4 Remove to the casserole dish or tagine you plan to use.
5 Add a little more oil to the frying pan and cook the onion for 5 minutes to soften.
6 Add the garlic and cook for another minute.
7 Add the cinnamon, ginger and cumin and stir through.
8 Put this mixture on top of the meat.
9 Now add the raisins or dried chopped apricots.
10 Cover with layers of carrots and potatoes, seasoning with salt and pepper between layers.

11 Melt the honey and mix it into the stock and pour the liquid over the contents of the dish, finishing with the last of the olive oil.

12 Cover the dish and bring the liquid to the boil, then turn down the heat to simmer on the stove or in the oven for 1½ hours or more, until the meat and vegetables are tender and the liquid is much reduced.

13 Scatter with the olives and coriander or parsley to serve.

SERVES 6

Chicken with lemon, olives and saffron

This is a comforting and tasty dish for cold winter days—it's my easy version of a chicken tagine. Serve it with couscous or bread and sprinkle with coriander leaves.

1 free-range chicken

For the stock
6 peppercorns
1 onion, cut into quarters
1 carrot
bunch of coriander stems

For the tagine
1 large red onion, grated
2 large cloves garlic, crushed
small bunch of fresh coriander, stems removed and reserved
100g unsalted butter
4 bay leaves
sea salt and black pepper

1 tspn ground cinnamon

1 tsp ground ginger

rind from 2 large preserved lemons, cut in wedges and rinsed, or two small
*   fresh lemons, quartered*

good pinch of saffron threads

handful of green olives

1 Joint the chicken into six portions.
2 To make the chicken stock put the backbone, wingtips and other bits of the chicken carcass in a large saucepan with the peppercorns, onion, carrot and coriander stems and cover with water. Bring to the boil and simmer for 40–60 minutes.
3 Meanwhile, place the chicken pieces in a large ovenproof dish or tagine dish—they should fit snugly without too many large gaps. Push the onion and garlic into the spaces between the chicken pieces.
4 In a small saucepan, stew the butter with the bay leaves, salt and pepper over a gentle heat for about 5 minutes—don't allow it to fry.
5 Set aside to cool and separate, then carefully strain the liquid over the chicken pieces and discard the solids.
6 Sprinkle the cinnamon and ginger over the contents of the casserole and stud the gaps with wedges of lemon.
7 Pour the stock around the chicken, to come halfway up the sides, then season to taste. (You may not need all the stock, but fresh stock is always handy or it can be frozen for later.)
8 Sprinkle the saffron into the liquid and cover the casserole dish, but leave an opening so the steam can escape, and set over a very low heat—so the liquid barely simmers—for about 1 hour. Alternatively, place a lid on the dish and cook in the oven preheated to 170°C for 1 hour.
9 Add the olives 5 minutes before the end of the cooking time.
10 Serve with a scattering of chopped coriander leaves.

SERVES 6

CHAPTER 22

At home with friends

It was early autumn back home in Governors Bay, New Zealand. The days were still—clear green seas and the dahlias, bright amongst lush garden foliage, were refreshed by late-summer rains. We celebrated the end of summer with family and an old friend and his new family, his third family really. As he commented, 'another life within *the other life*'. We spoke of trying to have as much as possible from life while we have the chance. I fully agreed with this philosophy, as we sat on the patio under the grape vines eating a late brunch. I was sorting some recipe books in preparation for this little event when a card fell out, a delightful handwritten message from a guest in appreciation of a cake I had given him for afternoon tea. He wrote, 'It was exquisite and to die for' . . . exuberant praise indeed. I felt I must find the recipe and try it again for our end-of-summer brunch.

I call this Morocco-inspired mint-syrup honeycake 'Cock-a-hoop honeycake' in honour of Margaret Mahy, borrowing the name from her delightful book *A Busy Day For A Good Grandmother*. Margaret loved this cake and we celebrated a few of her birthdays with this as the centrepiece. While it is a little fiddly to make, it is simple and always turns out well. You just need, as always, great ingredients and honey that isn't too highly flavoured. In New Zealand, I use clover or matagouri honey.

Cock-a-hoop honeycake

To get the texture for this cake just right, I like to buy the larger-cut thread coconut and use my food processor to make it a bit finer, but not as fine as desiccated coconut.

For the cake
160g butter, softened
310g sugar
2 tspn chopped fresh mint
200g flour
½ tspn baking powder
200g desiccated coconut
6 eggs, lightly beaten
40g ground almonds

For the syrup
200ml water
180g sugar
1 cup coarsely chopped fresh mint

For the topping
75g butter
180g honey
100g flaked almonds

1 Preheat the oven to 150°C. Line a 23cm springform cake tin with baking paper.
2 Beat the butter, sugar and mint until smooth.
3 Sieve the flour and baking powder together and stir in the coconut and ground almonds.
4 Add small quantities of the beaten eggs to the flour mixture, beating well after each addition to prevent the mixture from curdling.
5 Repeat until you have used all the ingredients and spread into the prepared tin.
6 Bake for 1 to 1½ hours. Check the cake is done by inserting a skewer in the centre. If it comes out clean the cake is ready.
7 Remove from the oven and allow to cool in the tin for 5 to 10 minutes.
8 While the cake is cooking, make the syrup by placing all the ingredients in a heavy-based saucepan and bringing to the boil, stirring occasionally to ensure the sugar is dissolved.
9 Remove from the heat and allow to cool for 30 to 45 minutes.
10 Strain through a sieve and discard the mint leaves.
11 Prick the warm cake all over with the skewer, then pour the syrup over the cake (which is still in the tin).
12 To make the topping, put the butter and honey in another small heavy-based saucepan and melt together.
13 Pour the topping over the cake and sprinkle with the almonds.
14 Place the cake back in the oven set at 170°C and bake for about 15 minutes, until the topping turns a light amber colour.
15 Allow the cake to cool in the tin for 20 to 30 minutes. While still warm, gently turn out onto a serving dish and remove the baking paper.

SERVES 12

The big long outdoor table, benches either side, was set under the grape vines groaning with fruit ready for another great dining occasion. We had a delicious menu from around the world, with influences and ideas collected from all our travel and from years of eating, adventuring and remembering, and enjoying the fruits of our garden.

From the home orchard, Peasgood's Nonsuch apples—the name so improbable and they are amazing 'cookers'—have been boiled to a soft pulp and mixed with fresh blueberries poached gently in syrup, served with yoghurt and cream and muesli. They are followed by frittata alle zucchini made with eggs fresh from the hens, courgettes from the garden and pancetta accompanied by quickly baked red and yellow baby tomatoes with the green tops and skin on.

All was accompanied by Pelorus sparkling wine, one of our favourites from the range of New Zealand sparkling white wines. To finish, we ate a slice of the Cock-a-hoop honeycake with cream or yoghurt and washed it down with a cup of tea or coffee.

Replete, I lay in the hot March sun with my grandchildren and caught up with our old friends while my son and daughter-in-law cleaned up the kitchen. Bliss!

Frittata alle zucchini

90g sliced pancetta or streaky bacon
625g sliced courgettes, diced into pieces
2 tbspn extra virgin olive oil
salt and freshly ground pepper
6 eggs, beaten

1 Lay the pancetta or bacon slices in a cast-iron skillet or heavy-based frying pan and cook over a low heat until crisp. Remove from the pan and crumble.

2 Put the courgettes in the pan, add the oil and cook over a medium heat until they begin to brown.

3 Sprinkle the crumbled pancetta or bacon over the courgettes and season with salt and pepper.

4 Pour the egg mixture into the hot zucchini and cook on one side, then tip the frittata onto a flat lid or plate and slide it back into the pan to cook the other side. Remove from the heat while the centre is still soft.

5 Transfer the frittata to a serving plate and serve immediately.

SERVES 6

Baked red and yellow cherry tomatoes

These are easy and don't take long to cook—you can put them in the oven towards the end of the cooking time to accompany many dishes, such as quiche, frittata, baked chicken and roast lamb.

red and yellow cherry tomatoes, if possible with the stalks attached (same number of each)
olive oil
rock salt

1 Place the tomatoes in a baking dish.

2 Splash a little olive oil over the tomatoes and sprinkle with some rock salt.

3 Bake in a medium to hot oven for a few minutes, until the tomatoes look cooked.

As my friend reminded me today, we are so lucky to have people to cook for. Here we are and we've travelled full circle—we've come of age with food, its availability, quality, variety and presentation. And the wines! We can be very satisfied with what's on offer down-under!

Our monthly wine order always used to include international wines. French if the occasion called for champagne and Australian if we're after a heavy rich red or, in the past, a pinot gris or maybe a verdhelo. We looked to France and Spain for rosé.

But now, we're happy with what's on offer at home and our order these days is mostly a mix of gorgeous New Zealand wines. Pinot noir, described as New Zealand's star red wine variety, late-harvest riesling, sauvignon blanc, pinot gris (also known as pinot grigio) and rich, buttery, smooth chardonnay. Locally produced verdhelo and viognier are fast expanding in this country. And we are lucky enough to enjoy particularly delicious wines from Argentina when the Argentine side of the family visits.

I try to cook for the season we're in, using the freshest produce on offer either from our own property or the local market—I find it is so satisfying. Not quite the French market or the Spanish or Italian, but the New Zealand-style Saturday Farmers' Market in Lyttelton, Christchurch. It's a wonderful social gathering with an eclectic mix of offerings, with pretty much consistent quality. We purchase for the week ahead, knowing we have the freshest and tastiest fruit and vegetables on offer, and meats regionally grown and prepared. I began to eat and enjoy pork again.

We had a dinner for five, and I celebrated the return to our lives of good pork by baking a pork rack in grape juice, accompanied by fresh figs from the garden marinated in red wine vinegar and sugar. Also on the menu that night was an entrée salad of tomato and fresh fennel and lemon and dessert, a Black Doris plum and apple tart. We topped off the evening with Belgian dark chocolate and ginger pieces in syrup, savouring the huge pleasure of home dining.

Lemon, tomato and fennel salad

I like the freshness of this combination . . . perfect as a small entrée or as a side salad on a very hot summer evening.

1 fennel bulb, finely sliced
4–6 tasty fresh tomatoes, finely chopped
2 lemons, zest and juice
2 tbspn olive oil
4 tspn mixed fresh chervil, parsley and basil, chopped
Salt
Ground pepper

1 Toss the fennel and tomatoes in a bowl with the lemon juice and olive oil.
2 Add the seasonings and lemon zest and fresh herbs and toss again.

SERVES 4

Pork rack with grape jelly and crisp baked sage

Buy a good-quality pork rack—the quality of the pork is essential to the taste of this simple dish. Allow one chop from the rack per serving, so ask the butcher to cut the rack to the size you need. I top the pork with grape jelly from the previous year's harvest, preserves and crisp-cooked sage.

1 pork rack, with 4 chops
salt
1½ cups red grape juice
handful of fresh sage leaves
olive oil
2 tbspn grape jelly

1 Preheat the oven to 180°C.
2 Sprinkle the pork rack liberally with salt and place it in a roasting dish.
3 Pour the grape juice over the meat.
4 Top with fresh sage leaves and a generous drizzle of olive oil.
5 Add the grape jelly to the liquid.
6 Bake until the meat juices run clear; pork does not usually have much juice to run clear. I usually see if the flesh looks white—how long will depend on how big the rack is. Do not overcook.
7 Cut the rack into separate pieces and let it stand in the grape and meat juices for a few minutes before serving.

SERVES 4

Black Doris plums baked with vanilla pod

Delicious to serve warm straight from the oven or cold later from the fridge for breakfast.

800g–1kg Black Doris plums, cleaned
2–3 cups sugar
1 vanilla pod

1 Preheat the oven to 160°C.
2 Cut the plums in half, discarding the stones, and place them in a single layer in a heavy ceramic baking dish, skin side down.
3 Cover with sugar.
4 Add the vanilla pod and enough water to prevent the plums from sticking—I start with ½ cup.
5 Put the uncovered dish in the oven for about 1 hour, until the juices are released and the plums begin to soften.

SERVES 6–8

On a visit to Sydney, 'just across the ditch' as we say here in New Zealand, I noticed that Sydney boasts the flavour of major Northern Hemisphere fashion and food spots, with its own special version, and the city exudes confidence. This place has a short but dynamic history—today, the world's rich and famous come to visit and live there and if you're into food and fashion it's definitely the place to be.

I was sitting at the Bather's Pavilion, a restaurant in Balmoral, where we made a toast 'to friendship and being alive'. My friend Miranda and I were enjoying the gorgeous environs of Balmoral by the sea, and the delicacies of the cuisine, when I overheard an elderly gentleman next to me savouring his dish: 'Oh, this sauce is delicious, it is divine!' he said and I found myself smiling at his pleasure.

Miranda and I had journeyed through the past two decades differently, mostly apart, but when our glasses of fine French champagne clinked and we offered the toast, there was a deep understanding and appreciation of our friendship. We toasted good friends and family—those we have, those we have lost, and those we never got to know. And to health—we are both survivors, as we reflect on our brushes with death and medical emergencies. And to passion, which makes it all more worthwhile. I noticed, once again, how I can be utterly transported when reflecting on life and living over a perfect meal. We acknowledged the mastery of the chef as we sampled our main courses—in my case on this occasion it was Humpty Doo barramundi. No, not a children's nursery rhyme, or a joke.

This is Sydney down-under and my delicious fillet of barramundi (an Australian fish) had been flown in from the Northern Territory, where it had been swimming in the waters of a place called Humpty Doo. Miranda's lamb had been trucked in from a southern state. We savoured our first tastes and reflected on the carbon footprint of our refined dining. Guilty? No, we're aging baby boomers, still trying to save the world, still capable of rationalising so we can have our cake and eat it, too. And I found myself, as always, torn between desire to have, to own, to taste, to experience more . . . or to be happy with what I already had.

CHAPTER 23

Beef, beef, glorious beef

San Carlos de Bariloche is the gem at the end of a huge journey across the Argentine interior. There is a new grandchild to greet, family gatherings and lots of delicious meat to eat. A previous trip to Buenos Aires had confirmed this, but this time a stay on the edge of Nahuel Huapi Lake, tucked underneath the majestic Andes and surrounded by a National Park, in the area known as Patagonia, just outside the township of San Carlos de Bariloche, totally cemented in my food memory banks the deliciousness of Argentine beef. There is no doubt—Argentina is the home of beautiful meat.

The environment here is beautiful, with huge expanses of virgin territory and a backdrop of enormous mountains. On a hot summer day, with a quiet wind gently moving through the giant beech trees and bees buzzing, it seems like paradise. There's the birth of a granddaughter with feasting and celebration. Even by European customs, family meals in Patagonia are late; the dinner sometimes is not served until 10.30 or even 11 at night.

Our Spanish almost non-existent, we struggled to communicate with the other grandparents, Abuela and Abu, as they are affectionately known by their family. With Abuela, I could communicate most easily in the kitchen. I was thrilled one day to find her preparing a huge and delicious-looking beef eye fillet in a very similar way to my beef coriander ginger recipe. Cilantro (coriander) was used liberally in her summer cooking. The beef was so tender, so fat free. Why is this? Is it because the beef cattle don't have to use much energy to get around as the ground is so flat, or is it the breed, or both? It's certainly a different experience eating beef here. When I sit down to a plate of Argentine beef, I'm so glad I'm not a vegetarian!

There was also a familiar potato dish (layers of potato) with liberal use of onion, pepper, salt and oil, gently fried then baked in a heavy earthenware dish.

These were very happy days. Raspberry canes on the property produced huge amounts of delicious fresh fruit daily and the delicious rich caramel-coloured dulce de leche, a bit thicker than the consistency of our sweetened condensed milk, was never absent from our evening meals. Some shops in Argentina were devoted entirely to the sale of this much-loved sweet treat.

Adriana's eye fillet beef

Ask your butcher to prepare a middle section for you, so all slices will be even. In Argentina this is very large indeed!

1 whole eye fillet, 900g–1kg
1 bunch of fresh coriander, roughly chopped (or parsley, as often used by
*   Adriana)*
½ cup olive oil
juice of 1 lime or lemon
4 cloves garlic

pepper and salt
extra fresh coriander, for serving

1 Take the meat fillet and slice lengthways to form a pocket, then place it in an oval baking dish. (Make sure it is a snug fit.)
2 Mix all the other ingredients and pour into the pocket and around the meat.
3 Marinate for several hours.
4 Preheat the oven to 220°C.
5 Bake the fillet for 10 minutes or more, depending on the size of the fillet and your guests' requirements for rare, medium or well done.
6 Take from the oven and cover with tinfoil. The beef will continue cooking while it rests.
7 Slice and serve, sprinkled with extra fresh coriander.

SERVES 6

This version of Adriana's recipe came from my friend Vicky in New Zealand. It has a few Asian-inspired additions and remains a favourite in our household.

3 tbspn grated fresh ginger
4 tbspn tamari sauce
1 or 2 small sweet red peppers, sliced finely for the addition of colour

Add these ingredients to Adriana's marinade mix and follow the same method.

Adriana's papas to go with the beef

6 large red-skinned potatoes, peeled and cut into 1cm slices
2 large red onions, thinly sliced
salt and pepper
¼ cup olive oil

1 Layer the potato and onion in a heavy baking dish, repeating the layers to finish with potato on top.
2 Season well and sprinkle with the olive oil.
3 Cook in a hot oven for 40 minutes or until the potatoes are cooked.

SERVES 6

Potatoes (papas), beef and dulce de leche in all its delicious forms are my recurring food memories of Argentina. Argentine legend suggests dulce de leche was discovered by accident, in the early 1800s, when a forgetful maid left sweetened milk on the stove, returning to find it transformed into a delicious creamy mixture. It's included in the book *1001 Foods You Must Taste Before You Die*, so you don't just have to take my word for it!

Dulce de leche

Dulce de leche, described by some as 'an ambrosial milk jam', is a slow-boiled mix of milk and sugar, often enhanced with vanilla and bicarbonate of soda.

3 litres milk
1 tspn bicarbonate of soda
1kg sugar, dissolved in ½ litre of hot water
1 vanilla bean

1 Using a heavy-based saucepan, bring the milk and soda to the boil.
2 Add the sugar syrup and vanilla bean.
3 Stir slowly with a wooden spoon for about 50 minutes, over medium to low heat, until the colour changes to a darker creamy yellow.
4 When this process is complete, remove from the heat but keep stirring continuously until the mixture cools. If you want to hasten the process, place the saucepan into a sink of cold water while stirring.

MAKES APPROX 3 CUPS

CHAPTER 24

The art of cooking

Despite the huge number of cookbooks on sale, glossy magazines luring us to buy them and salivate as we fantasise over each mouth-watering dish on display, and endless TV cooking shows, there are millions who have access to food and a kitchen yet don't have the knowledge, skill, confidence or drive to make their own delicious meals. The efforts to encourage people to cook 'healthy' meals for themselves and their family are endless, some of the best examples coming from the imaginative and energetic Jamie Oliver, but the fact remains, all over the world people leave the supermarket with food they are ill-equipped to turn into appetising meals.

This week I was visited by a young woman who had arrived in New Zealand from Brazil three years ago and stayed with us for 18 months, assisting me during my recovery from a head injury. In February 2004 I developed a subdural bleed after an accident while dancing at a wedding, with two subsequent surgeries to save my life. Michelle was remembering how, when she arrived, not only did she not have English language skills, but she also had little knowledge of food and its preparation. While she had been raised with her mother and grandmother's country cooking, when she moved to the city and life in an apartment in Rio de Janeiro, she had left those customs behind and she and her flatmates had hardly ever eaten at home. But arriving in New Zealand, Michelle became an avid student of home-making. She was like a sponge and quickly soaked up both the English language and the art of food preparation, and I benefited from her meticulous help around the home, especially in the kitchen.

As we sat eating lunch together on a gorgeous warm weekday afternoon under the newly leafed grape vine, eating our favourite fresh lemon cake, which has been part of my repertoire for twenty-five years, she told me how happy she was to have learnt about food preparation and presentation. Michelle has since completed her studies to become a chef and is working at one of New Zealand's most highly regarded boutique hotels, The George, here in Christchurch.

Fresh lemon cake

This is my famous lemon cake recipe, a staple in my repertoire because it is quick to make and delicious to eat. It's also delicious made with oranges or limes or a combination, and can provide a base for fresh partially cooked and sweetened plums, apples, apricots—whatever fruit is in season. Just drop the cooked fruit into the batter when it is in the cake tin. By using partially cooked fruit you will avoid having the fruit and the cake cooking at different times and retain the intense colour of the fruit. I like to use the oven bake method for cooking the fruit to retain the strongest flavours. For a special occasion, double the recipe and forget about waiting for the cake to cool—enjoy this while it's still warm. It freezes well, but you'll need to freeze it without the syrup and when the cake has thawed reheat it and pour hot syrup over the cake just before serving.

For the cake

115g butter, softened
zest of 1 lemon
170g plain flour
1 tspn baking powder
170g caster sugar
2 eggs
3 tbspn milk, approximately (or 1 tbspn of acidophilus yoghurt and 2
*   tbspn milk)*

For the topping

55g granulated sugar
juice of 2 lemons

1   Preheat the oven to 180°C. Line the base of a 20cm cake tin with baking paper.
2   To make the cake, put all the ingredients in a bowl and, using an electric mixer, beat together.
3   Pour the mixture into the prepared tin and bake for 40 to 50 minutes. Remove from the oven and leave in the tin to cool.
4   Meanwhile, prepare the topping by mixing the sugar and juice together to form a thick paste.
5   While the cake is still hot, sprinkle the topping over the cake.
6   Allow the cake to cool a little before serving.

SERVES 6–8

People often say they live alone so they can't really be bothered about food. It really shouldn't matter if there's one to feed or ten—the basics remain the same. Purchasing or growing good-quality produce, creating a meal, simple or complicated—whatever you have the time for—the rules remain unchanged. And, of course, allowing time and choosing a place in which to savour your food, whether it's at a table, in a corner at work, outside under a tree, in front of the TV from a tray, around a kitchen table or in a formal dining area, it really doesn't matter. What does matter is that you have participated in the gathering and preparation in some way, you smell the food cooking, you understand where it came from and you celebrate the joy of it when you finally get to eat it.

As a very welcome post-earthquake respite, I stayed with my friend Barb in Hobart. It had been three months since the second major earthquake that had devastated Christchurch on 22 February 2011. It brought massive destruction and terror, with 185 lives lost. Our family's homes and our business premises were severely damaged. Leaving the city for some respite was important. Arriving in Hobart, thirty years after our initial meeting, I enjoyed Barb's home-making skills once again. She now lives alone, yet maintains the same quality in her meals as when she was feeding a family every day and crowds of friends often. Again I'm inspired by the tastes fresh from her kitchen and the balance in her meals. I take away delicious memories of grilled quail, spiced quince jelly and an old tried-and-true recipe for tomato chutney. I'm an avid student of hers, once again, soaking up her years of experience.

Barb's grilled quail

This is delicious with spiced Quince jelly (see page 209).

4 quails
2 tbspn olive oil (more if required)

1 tbspn tamari or other good soy sauce
2 tbspn honey
zest of 1 orange
pepper and salt

1 To butterfly each quail, place the bird on a chopping board with the backbone on top. Cut down each side of the backbone with a very sharp knife, and remove it and use it for stock. Turn the bird over and push down so that it lies flat. (Some people also remove the breastbone, but I leave it in. Barb purchases them already butterflied.)
2 Make the marinade by mixing the remaining ingredients together.
3 Place the birds breast side up in a baking dish and pour the marinade over the birds.
4 Marinate for at least 2 hours.
5 Grill the quail for a few minutes on each side or bake in the oven at 200°C for 15 to 20 minutes, depending on the size of the birds.

SERVES 2

Mrs Campbell's tomato chutney

The Campbells were an early colonial Scottish family who owned the Nant Estate in Bothwell, Tasmania. Barb remembers visits there and it was from one of these that she aquired Mrs Campbell's prized chutney recipe.

30g white peppercorns
30g whole cloves
7g allspice berries

3.5kg tomatoes, peeled and chopped
4 large apples, peeled and chopped
3 large onions, peeled and chopped
1 cup sultanas
650g sugar
60g salt
1 litre apple cider vinegar

1 Tie the peppercorns, cloves and berries in a muslin bag.
2 Put together with the remaining ingredients in a large heavy-based saucepan, bring to the boil and simmer for 3 hours.
3 Remove the spice bag and ladle the chutney into hot sterilised jars and seal.

MAKES ABOUT 12 SMALL JARS

When doing my monthly shop for staples of olive oil, tomato products and hard cheeses at a local Mediterranean importers, I was impressed to meet up with an older woman, basket on her arm, confidently ordering orecchiette and pancetta. I watched her, interested in the ingredients she was ordering and wondering, in my usual way, what she was going to cook. I finally asked her and she described the pasta she was going to create that night, adding, 'I can cook what I like, you know, I live alone now with my husband having passed away last year.' She reconfirmed for me that food, its collection and its preparation, can be an inspiring and comforting experience for all ages.

Orecchiette with pancetta and mozzarella

Inspired by the woman able to cook what she likes.

250g orecchiette
2 slices pancetta
6 tbspn olive oil
*200g fresh cherry or grape tomatoes (round or pear shaped) in assorted
    colours*
125g fresh buffalo mozzarella, cut into small chunks
3 tbspn white wine vinegar
1 clove garlic, crushed
3 tbspn chopped chives
2 tbspn chopped oregano

1 Cook pasta in a large saucepan of boiling salted water until tender, stirring occasionally.
2 In a pan, fry the pancetta in a little of the oil.
3 Halve the tomatoes and cut the mozzarella into small chunks.
4 Drain the pasta, then tip into a warm serving bowl. Add the chunks of mozzarella.
5 Add all of the other ingredients and toss well. Serve immediately.

SERVES 2

We are fortunate in New Zealand to have a huge choice of edible things to buy and, for many of us, a bit of soil and a good climate in which to grow some or all of our own food. It's amazing how many vegetables you can grow, even in a wooden tub, when outdoor space is limited. There is a wide range of food outlets to suit every taste and budget, and it's up to us what we do with all this choice.

So, how do we define the art of food preparation and presentation? In my mind, the priority is not how beautiful or artistic it looks on the plate, although this aspect can definitely be an added bonus. To me, it's about the overall experience, the ambience, and that starts with obtaining the best-quality ingredients. There's very little even a good cook can do when presented with poor ingredients. Look for the freshest and the tastiest of whatever you are buying—with fruit and veges this often means avoiding the largest produce on offer. If you want flavour, organic, more naturally grown, will generally be a bit smaller and not perfectly formed but most often it will be full of flavour. Spray free is often an alternative to organic when trying to cut the price. Buy fresh, the freshest you can get in season, and choose each ingredient with care. From the moment of selection to the final presentation to the table, there needs to be a connection between you and the food you are preparing. It doesn't have to be elaborate or time consuming, but there must be an ongoing commitment to quality. A dish I often cook that meets these criteria is a sausage ragout—the vital ingredient is a high-quality pork or beef sausage without preservatives or colouring and some acid-free tomato pulp.

Sausage ragout

I like to use pork, sage and apple or Italian spicy pork sausages for this tasty dish that certainly dresses up the sausages.

3 tbspn olive oil
2 red onions, finely sliced
3 cloves garlic, chopped
550g sausages
1 cup red wine
2 × 400g cans chopped tomatoes
fresh oregano and thyme
2 bay leaves
salt and freshly ground black pepper

1 Heat the oil in a heavy-based frying pan and add the onions and garlic. Fry gently until clear.
2 Add the chopped sausages and don't worry about the meat that squeezes out of the skins.
3 Brown the sausages and any crumbled sausage meat.
4 Add the wine and cook, stirring, until the wine is absorbed.
5 Add the tomatoes, herbs and bay leaves and season to taste.
6 Place a lid on the pan and simmer on the stove top or pour into an ovenproof dish with a lid and bake for 30 minutes at 180°C.

SERVES 6

One night I stood in line at a local fish and chip shop with a granddaughter who wanted chips. We chose a very bad time—early Friday evening is when many people order their weekly takeaway treat. The thought of buying fish and chips was attractive at first but soon faded as I stood in the queue, so I asked for one quick scoop of chips (to keep hunger pangs at bay) and three fresh uncooked fillets to take home. Everyone was happy. Hot chips to nibble on, while at home on the grill the fish was cooked with tomatoes and sweet red peppers.

Grilled blue cod with red peppers and tomatoes

olive oil
1 red pepper, deseeded and cut into strips
2 tomatoes, halved
butter
2 blue cod fillets

1 Heat a grill plate and sprinkle it with olive oil.
2 Quickly sear the red pepper and tomatoes. Set aside and keep warm.
3 Put a small amount of butter and a sprinkle of oil on the grill plate and sear the fish fillets on both sides.
4 Cook for a few minutes until the fish is cooked through.
5 Serve with red peppers, tomatoes and home-made potato chips.

SERVES 2

My friend Alison, who lives in Noosa, continues to be a food mentor. Over the years we have traded food tips and shared countless meals. She has taught me the secrets of fine food on a budget and is equally at home on the gourmet trail. Armed with *Gourmet Traveller*'s best restaurant guide, Alison met me during one of my many trips to Brisbane. We manage sampling from menus in two recommended restaurants one night and a third the next, freezing in over-zealous air-conditioning. On another occasion a fire alarm forces us to abandon our restaurant seats altogether, but not before Alison samples her crocodile main.

Alison's home-made potato chips

Make chips with clean potatoes and you can either leave the skins on—they'll be easier to make and be more nutritious—or peel them. Allow enough potatoes per person and then some, according to appetite.

potatoes
extra virgin olive oil
chopped garlic, according to taste
Maldon sea salt
handful of fresh rosemary chopped

1 Preheat the oven on fan setting to 200°C.
2 Chop the potatoes into good-sized fingers and place them in a plastic bag.
3 Drizzle extra virgin olive oil into the bag and toss the chips to ensure they are all coated with oil. Tip the chips into a roasting pan and sprinkle with lots of chopped garlic and Maldon salt.
4 Place the pan in the preheated oven.
5 Keep an eye on the chips and turn over to brown on the other side.

Back to the blue cod I bought from the chip shop. Avocado was quickly prepared into a version of guacamole for a meal that was full of flavour, served with chips, chopped parsley, lemon wedges and a green salad—all from the garden. For dessert we had fresh raspberries and a dribble of cream.

Once you're confident of turning whatever you have in your cupboard, fridge, freezer or garden into a tasty meal, that is when you begin to learn the art of food preparation.

Raspberry fool

This is the easiest dessert to make and, served in pretty glasses, it looks impressive. If you use frozen berries it will be ready to serve straightaway.

2 punnets fresh raspberries (or 4½ cups frozen)
sugar to taste
2 cups cream

1 Purée the fresh berries or thaw the frozen berries.
2 Sprinkle the berries with sugar to taste.
3 Whip the cream, not too stiff, and carefully fold in the berries.
4 Spoon the mixture into serving dishes.
5 Cover and keep in the fridge until ready to serve immediately.

SERVES 6

CHAPTER 25

Fungi fever

With all the dampness and warmth in the gardens have come fungi. Suddenly, there's passionate discussion about boletus, cèpes and porcini (they are one and the same). *Boletus edulis*, a European forest mushroom that has been introduced to New Zealand, is highly prized so eyes light up, stories flow and the hunt is on. I reflected on our advanced fungi education in France and Italy, filling out my very rudimentary knowledge about eating mushrooms gained during my childhood in the 1950s. Certainly, nobody called them fungi then!

There was a definite suspicion in my family of anything other than common field mushrooms. It took a lot of persuasion to entice me to actually try some of the other delicacies the world of fungi has to offer—boletus, girolle (also known as golden chanterelle), trompette de la mort (also known as the horn of plenty and black chanterelle), and morel.

I connected most readily to boletus. Mark became a devotee of this delicacy, and collecting it has become an annual hobby. I laughed as I listened to the manager of a local specialist food outlet talking with my husband about a 'cowboy' porcini collector. They were upset about his methods as he took them too young and too small, ruining it for other collectors. They discussed in detail the merits of cutting the stem at certain heights from the base, and the possibility of the local council fencing off certain trees to allow more porcini to grow!

This discussion reminded me of our time in France in early autumn in the Dordogne. The owners of the property we were staying at were away and we had been left with a number of instructions. Some of them we didn't understand the signicance of until locals started showing up at the door. What an experience!

For the previous week conditions had been perfect and the forests all around us had begun to produce fungi of all descriptions. The fungi books were out to aid with identification and by the second day both fridges were bursting. By the third day, the housekeeper had received a large supply with a request for her to preserve them. Then the telephone began to ring and ring and the doorbell, too, as more and more requests poured in to collect the edible treasures.

The locals read the signs posted up in the forests surrounding the house: 'Stop—Prosecution Follows. Please make contact with the owners of the house.' They realised years of free access to the property were over and they must apply to the household for permission to collect the edible fungi.

Their passion for fungi was amazing and it was as if they were led by an overwhelming compulsion. They sniffed the air and realised the time was right, their tastebuds on fire with anticipation. No one is exempt—this fever affects the local policeman, the door-to-door salesman, the Limoges china dealer from the local market and the local fireman. It seems to capture most of the adult population of nearby villages—all are reduced to the same level and they are helpless to the need for fungi! Their eyes dance with anticipation. They bribe. They invent stories and elaborate excuses as to why they should have access.

Returning from a bike ride I noticed gendarmes parked just inside the gate, presumably to catch speeding drivers. Evidently, it's something they do quite often. Their moustaches twitched and eyes lit up as we biked past with our bags full, this time not with mushrooms, but with figs, grapes and blackberries. Lots more requests came in. All day I saw the gendarmes parked in their van, but I didn't see them catch even one speeding driver. They appeared to be waiting for an opportunity to go into the forest, but our continued presence in the garden prevents them from foraging for fungi.

Police weren't the only uniformed visitors that week. We noticed uniformed officials from the neighbouring hunting agency on the property, but the hunting season is still two weeks away. It has to be the call of the champignons. After that, foraging for fungi—ceps in particular, collecting, preparing and consuming them—is now an important part of our annual rhythm. Two of our adult children are now avid enthusiasts and competitiveness and secretiveness about collection sites seems to have become part of the process, even within the family.

We experimented with new recipes and revisited old favourites, including potato ceps pie. Another more recent addition is sauce for meat that my new friend Katerina, or Katie, from the Czech Republic gave me. She is so excited when she sees a basket of fresh ceps come home with Mark. 'So you have these, too,' she exclaimed. 'These are gorgeous.' She told me about her grandmother's cooking, and ways of cooking ceps or porcini with which she has grown up. I followed her instructions and made her grandmother's sauce on the spot. I found myself an immediate convert.

Katie's grandmother's porcini sauce

The most unusual ingredient here is the caraway seeds. Rather than diminish the flavour of the fungi, they enhance it. This sauce is delicious with meat or on its own as an entrée, with a piece of warm crusty bread to soak up the juices.

3–4 medium-sized porcini
30g butter
pinch of salt
150ml cream
small pinch of caraway seeds to taste (optional)
50ml chicken stock (increase to 100ml for a thinner sauce)

1 Clean the fresh porcini and slice the stems.
2 Fry the stems gently in the butter, then add the sliced caps.
3 Add the salt, cream and caraway seeds, if using.
4 Stir and cook for 10 minutes or until the mixture tastes cooked.

MAKES ABOUT 300ML

Potato and porcini pie

I have memories of making this in a heavy cast-iron pan on an open fire during a power cut in the Dordogne one year.

If you don't have porcini, you can make this with flat brown mushrooms. In France duck fat is readily available but at home in New Zealand I use butter. Just a note about ridding fungi of worms: I usually try to cut them out but sometimes end up losing a lot of mushroom, so if you put them into a hot oven on a tray for a few minutes, the worms may leave fast.

2 tbspn duck fat or butter
3 large potatoes, peeled and thinly sliced
2–3 ceps, sliced
2 cloves garlic, chopped
sea salt and freshly ground black pepper
young fresh parsley, finely chopped

1 Heat a heavy-based frying pan and add the duck fat or butter and the potatoes. Brown the potato slices.
2 Add the sliced mushroom caps, then the chopped stems and the garlic.
3 Season and allow to simmer over a very low heat. Continue cooking until the potato is soft.
4 Sprinkle with finely chopped parsley before serving.

SERVES 4

Dining one evening at Lisa and Yommi's Saggio di Vino, a celebrated local restaurant, with a group of American clients, Lisa, the restaurant owner was proudly showing a large, fresh New Zealand-grown black truffle—it's the size of a small golf ball. The waitress was grating the precious truffle for our table when she suddenly lost control and dropped it. It rolled away across the tiled floor as we all watched, mesmerised.

From where she was standing, Lisa surveyed its final resting place beneath the raised heel of a diner's foot. He was agitated, leaning forward and trying to select the right moment, it appeared, to propose. He was at a very delicate part of proceedings while another delicate moment of significant economic proportions was taking place directly under his raised heel.

Lisa pounced as if catching a wild animal. She grabbed at the truffle just before the heel of his shoe came down. Lifting it high in the air, like a prized trophy, she announced, 'And if you think I'm going to wash it, you're mistaken. It is a lot cleaner on my floor than where it came from.' We were all astonished as she whisked it out to the kitchen for a quick wipe down with a dry cloth before returning it to the waitress.

George Biron, a Melbourne restaurateur, was coming to Christchurch to see if *Boletus edulis* was growing here. To his knowledge, it wasn't growing in Australia. Another well-known chef, cookery writer and fellow restaurateur Stephanie Alexander, had asked him to follow up for her on a rumour. Mark had been quoted in *Cuisine* as a bit of an expert on boletus here in Christchurch. George went off on daily forays, bringing fungi back to his hotel, and Mark was invited to view them. Arriving at George's hotel room, Mark was astonished to see the spare bed stripped down to the bottom sheet and a large assortment of fungi, not including *Boletus edulis* I have to say, arranged on the once-white sheet. It wasn't very hard to imagine the horrified reactions of the cleaning staff when George checked out, demonstrating, once again, how all rationality goes when the hunt is on for fungi.

Seven years ago, Mark had his first successful boletus inoculation under the silver birch trees here at Ribbonwood. For the last three to four years we have been harvesting a few boletus each season!

Quick-fried ceps

Quickly pan fried, freshly picked ceps are a wonderful way to start your evening. It's our favourite way to prepare them, served with some bread to mop up the juices and a glass of soft merlot or malbec or, if you prefer white wine, an oaky New Zealand chardonnay.

butter
oil
crushed garlic to taste
freshly picked ceps, dewormed if necessary and cut into very thin slices
salt

1 In a heavy-based frying pan, heat a little butter, oil and crushed garlic.
2 When the pan is very hot, add batches of the ceps slices and a sprinkle of salt.
3 Turn them over so they colour on both sides and quickly remove onto a warm serving platter.
4 This process will take 1 minute or less per batch. Serve immediately.

Sauce forestière

While this sauce sounds very indulgent and fiddly to make, it is an absolutely delicious accompaniment to meat. It can also be made with 150g of fresh forest fungi, sliced and thrown straight into the pan.

50g dried morel or ceps, or a mixture of the two
small knob of butter
2–4 shallots, sliced

2 cloves garlic
1 sprig of thyme
150ml madeira
150ml beef stock
500ml cream
salt and pepper

1 Soak the fungi in 500ml of warm water for 30 minutes. Squeeze out the excess water and set the fungi aside.
2 Melt the butter in a heavy-based saucepan and gently fry the shallots, garlic and thyme.
3 Add the madeira, the soaking liquid from the fungi and the beef stock and keep at a low simmer, stirring until the mixture reduces by half.
4 Add the cream and continue heating. Season to taste, remove from the heat and set aside to cool.
5 Blend this mixture and then put through a fine sieve.

SERVES 4

CHAPTER 26

Autumn harvest at Ribbonwood

My diary captured the comparatively tranquil months of early 2010, six months before the first earthquake. Easter came early. A full moon ensured the most perfect late-March weather and it's my favourite time of year. At our place on the Bay came the pure white anemones we call Lent lilies and roses—the very sweetly scented Margaret Merrill. The sea was green and still. In the garden was the cooing of white pigeons and the contented swooshing of kereru (native wood pigeons) as they landed in the puriri tree to gobble the ripening fruit. The white tablecloths were on the tables and Easter feasting began.

For Good Friday afternoon tea there were hot cross buns made by a chef who lives locally, and they're as I remember from childhood—you won't find colourings or preservatives in these delicious buns.

Later, dinner took place over a stimulating conversation re the merits, or otherwise, of a carbon-credit system to help alleviate the problems of global warming. The ongoing debate continued as we munched our way through an entrée of fresh tomatoes from the garden, sweet and small, grown with little water, resulting in an intense flavour, sprinkled with fresh basil, drizzled with balsamic and olive oil and eaten with hot rosemary bread.

The conversation continued, our visitor exclaiming with despair that our world had gone mad. She described a scheme to plant large areas of deforested Amazonian rainforest in central Brazil with Australian eucalypts.

'Well, would you rather see soya beans or eucalypts?'

'Which of these will be more useful as carbon converters?'

I could see the host going into overdrive to defend his position.

We started our main course—eye fillet steak marinated in tamari and ginger sauce on a bed of baked red peppers, accompanied by a gratin of potato and kumara.

The dessert that followed was a quince and apple tarte Tatin (see page 136), made with the first quince of the season fresh-picked from the tree that hung heavy with perfumed golden fruits. I finally learnt where the word Tatin comes from—it was sisters of the Tatin family from the Loire area who invented this upside-down apple pie that is so much a part of French tradition and now a much-loved dessert worldwide.

After Easter, perfect harvest weather continued, still hot and clear, and it was time for the grape harvest from the pergola on the terrace. This year my team was all female. It's a first—there are usually more male helpers than female, but that was not possible this year as we'd chosen a mid-week picking day and Michelle and her Brazilian vineyard worker friends were all working elsewhere. As always, we stopped for a harvest lunch surrounded by baskets brimming with black grapes. It was a good pick.

Lunch was a freshly made bacon and egg pie with hot, new season's plum sauce, accompanied by a still-warm rosemary flat bread and a tomato salad. Dessert was a slow-baked quince, with a scoop of vanilla ice cream and leftover slices of Cock-a-hoop honeycake (see page 167) from the freezer. Everyone was happy and full of joie de vivre, any physical tiredness restored by the camaraderie and the hearty lunch. There were more than 60 kilograms of grapes to deal with and so began the process of preparing grape jelly and juice.

The jelly this year is clear and deep purple and it set easily. It's perfect for pouring over a chicken, glazing a roasting leg of lamb or a rack of pork. In fact, it's the perfect ingredient for many long, slow-cooking meat dishes. The grape juice is also perfect for a marinade. I felt satisfied as the shelves in the kitchen and pantry began to look full of promise of many good meals to come during the winter months ahead.

Hot cross buns

These are full of natural sweetness from the spice and dried fruit.

20g yeast or 1 capful
3 tbspn sugar
½ cup warm water
½ cup warm milk
450g plain flour
70g butter
1 tbspn mixed spice
2 eggs, beaten
70g currants
70g sultanas

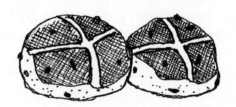

For the egg wash
1 egg
3ml milk

For the glaze

⅓ cup water
2 tbsp sugar

For the crosses

3 tbspn flour
water to mix flour to a thin paste

1 Dissolve the yeast and 1 tbspn of the sugar in the warm water and milk until it begins to foam (about 15 minutes).
2 Put the flour in a large bowl and add the butter.
3 Rub the butter into the flour, then add the rest of the sugar and the spice.
4 Mix in the eggs and the yeast mixture and stir until it forms a dough.
5 Knead until smooth, then add in the dried fruit.
6 Knead a bit longer and then place the dough ball in a bowl, cover with a tea towel and leave in a warm place to rise until doubled in size.
7 Knead again and shape into buns—this should make between 16 and 18 buns. Place the buns on a greased and floured baking tray and set aside to rise for about 1 hour.
8 Preheat the oven to 200°C.
9 To make the egg wash, whisk the egg and milk together then brush the buns with the egg wash.
10 For the crosses, put the flour and water paste into a piping bag, or use a plastic bag and cut the corner to make a piping bag.
11 Pipe crosses onto the buns and bake for 10 to 15 minutes.
12 To make the glaze, in a heavy-based saucepan heat the water and sugar until the sugar dissolves.
13 When you take the buns from the oven, brush with the sugar glaze.

MAKES 16–18 BUNS

Harvester's bacon and egg pie

I prefer to use a lean back bacon, but any good bacon will do.

1 prepared pastry shell (see Perfect shortcrust pastry, page 46)

For the filling
3–4 slices bacon
6 eggs
75ml milk
75ml cream
pepper and salt
chopped parsley
2 handfuls frozen peas (optional)

1 Preheat the oven to 200°C.
2 Arrange the bacon in a single layer on the unbaked pastry shell.
3 In a bowl, beat the eggs, milk, cream and seasonings and pour the mixture into the pastry shell.
4 Scatter the peas into the eggy mixture, if using peas.
5 Bake for 20 to 30 minutes until the pastry looks cooked and the egg mixture has risen.
6 Serve with Spiced plum sauce (see page 206) and salad.

SERVES 6

Spiced plum sauce

This is a pantry staple that I make each year when plums are in season. It is very tasty and hot, but not chilli hot!

3kg plums, destoned
1kg brown sugar
1.5 litres white vinegar
3 red onions
3 tspn salt
3 tspn ground cloves
2 tspn allspice
1 tspn ground pepper
50g piece fresh ginger or 2 tspn ground ginger
2 tspn ground nutmeg
2 tspn ground mustard seeds
½ tspn turmeric

1 Combine all the ingredients in a preserving pan, bring to the boil and simmer for 1 hour.
2 Blend the cooked ingredients into a smooth sauce and pour into clean, sterilised glass bottles and seal.

MAKES APPROXIMATELY 4 LITRES (OR 6 × 670ML PASSATA JARS)

Grape jelly

Some years this jelly sets better than others. I think the quicker you get the grapes from the vines and prepared for cooking the better the result. I usually make two or three batches of this per season, using in total about 25 kilograms of grapes.

6kg grapes
2kg cooking apples, unpeeled and chopped into quarters
water
2 cups sugar to every 2½ cups strained grape and apple liquid
juice of 2 lemons

1 Wash the bunches of grapes and remove the grapes from the stalks.
2 Put them into a large preserving pan (I use a 36cm diameter pan) and add the chopped cooking apples (skins cores and all)—about one-third of the volume of grapes.
3 Almost cover the fruit with water and bring to the boil. Continue simmering gently until the grape skins are bursting and the liquid is a rich purple.
4 Strain overnight through a jelly bag. If you are in a hurry, you can strain the liquid and carry on. Although the resulting jelly will taste fine it won't be as clear.
5 Measure the resulting liquid and put back in the pan, stirring in 2 cups of sugar for every 2½ cups of liquid.
6 Add the lemon juice and boil rapidly until setting point is reached. To test for setting I usually turn the heat off and leave the jelly in the pan to cool. If when it cools it has a skin and becomes jelly like in appearance I know it has reached a setting point. Sometimes this can even be left overnight in the pan. If the jelly is proving difficult to set I add a whole lemon and sometimes a whole apple and simmer a little longer with the whole fruit in the mixture to help the setting. When you are ready to put into the jars reheat to simmer point and bottle into hot sterilised jars. Another testing method from my friend Maria, who makes a great plum jelly, is to put a saucer in the freezer to chill. Then take a teaspoon

of the hot mixture and place on the saucer. Leave for about 10 minutes, and if there is some setting occurring it is ready to put into jars.

MAKES ABOUT 6 × 670ML JARS

It was 10 April, the night before my youngest son's birthday, a truly gorgeous time of the year as the season flowed from late summer to autumn, with a hint of winter in the early morning air. Tonight, two heavy saucepans on the stove were cooking golden quinces, spreading their highly perfumed aroma through the house. As the colours changed from golden to pinkish to a rich red, jelly formed in the pans. I use two wonderful old recipes to make quince jelly and quince paste, both easy and sure to please.

Quince paste

This will last all winter and is a wonderful treat with bread and cheese when you need a burst of energy.

fresh quinces
1 lemon
water
sugar
caster sugar

1 Wipe the quinces, then cut first into quarters and then eighths and remove the core.

2 Put the fruit in a heavy saucepan with the lemon juice and enough water to cover the fruit.

3 Cover and simmer 30 to 40 minutes until the fruit is soft.

4 Press all the fruit and juice in the pan through a sieve to render a thick purée. This requires a lot of patience.

5 Weigh the purée and for each 500g, add the same weight of sugar.

6 Cook over a low heat for a long time, stirring constantly until thick. This will take at least an hour, and sometimes even longer.

7 Turn into shallow metal trays lined with greaseproof paper.

8 Cover with a light cloth for 4 to 5 days in a warm place.

9 When it has set firmly, cut into small slices and dust with caster sugar.

10 Store in airtight containers.

Quince jelly

This looks and tastes wonderful. Sometimes, I add pieces of slow-baked quince (see below) to the jelly when putting it into jars—rich coloured pieces of quince suspended in a deep red jelly are my favourite preserve.

2kg sugar
3 litres water
6 large ripe quinces
juice of 2 lemons

1 Put the sugar and water in a heavy-based saucepan and stir to dissolve the sugar.

2 Wipe the furry coating from the quinces and put them in a large pan.

3 Pour the syrup over the quinces.

4 Gradually bring this to a boil and continue boiling until almost setting.

5 Add the lemon juice and continue to simmer until setting point. See Grape jelly notes (page 207) for setting point.
6 Remove the quinces. The jelly left in the pan is now ready for putting into warm sterilised jars. Add 12 black peppercorns, 2 star anise and 2 cinnamon quills to the quinces as they cook to make spiced quince jelly for a condiment that is especially good with roasted meats.

MAKES 8–10 MEDIUM SIZED JARS

Slow-baked quince

1½ cups sugar
2 cups water
zest of 2 lemons
4 perfect unbruised quince, cleaned but unpeeled

1 Preheat the oven to 170°C.
2 Make a syrup by heating the sugar, water and lemon zest in a heavy-based saucepan until the sugar has dissolved.
3 Cut the quinces in half and remove the cores.
4 Lie the quinces cut-side down in a heavy baking dish.
5 Pour over enough syrup to almost cover the fruit.
6 Cover with tinfoil and bake for 1 to 2 hours, until the fruit becomes very pink and soft.

SERVES 4–6

The quince jelly with chunks of the slow-baked quince has become the preferred accompaniment for our breakfast yoghurt and it's a favourite with all ages. Some people have become addicted to this quince treat. One friend in particular took a jar home and hid it from her family, and she confessed to eating it all at one sitting in a moment of depression. That must have been some sweet hit! As the quinces are simmering away, I lit the wood stove and the cat and dog cuddled up together, enjoying the luxury of their warm bed. Outside the air had that delicious wood-smoke aroma. Winter wasn't far away.

CHAPTER 27

Comfort food

It was 2008. As one of the youngest of the post-war baby boom I was faced with sadness and concern for an aging parent—a delicate mother, fussy with her food, faced with having to go into full-time hospital care. A stupid accident and frail health had taken her from her home, where she loved her independence and being able to make her own choices. What could I do for my mother in these hospital situations, first public and later private, except be her advocate, her comfort, and do something very practical, which comforted both of us? I would cook for her. Even if she only had three or four spoonfuls, at least the tastes, flavours and smells were delicious—I determined to provide her with food prepared with love and attention to detail, for her particular needs as a very frail elderly person.

For days and weeks those of us who loved her and were closest to her lived in a strange 'other world', the world of intense hospital visiting. Add to that the disruption of not being in our own home town and you had a recipe for distressed caregivers. I found the exercise of buying the ingredients and cooking them in my mother's kitchen gave me some warmth and connection to her otherwise empty home, where I was staying.

My mother's increasing frailty and diminishing size caused concern. Dieticians were called. An omelette was especially made in the kitchen, but when it arrived it was large and tough—the size alone was enough to deter a delicate eater. It was no surprise that it was refused. 'No dear, I will not eat that—it is not how I like it, not how I know it,' she said, very firmly.

I saw very quickly that if my mother was ever going to eat again during her recovery from pneumonia and a broken hip, it wasn't going to be hospital food. I started to cook for her again. Every time I cooked for her, I ate as well. The only difference was, I had to purée her food—what the hospital staff call 'texture modified' food—but I was careful to purée things separately so she was presented with a colourful selection rather than a dull sludge at mealtimes.

Some of her favourite dishes were pumpkin and coconut cream soup with plenty of fresh chicken stock, sprinkled with coriander, and I also made potato and kumara baked with butter to add extra calories. Coconut chicken—chicken breasts poached in coconut cream and lemon zest—also went down well, as did chicken poached in orange juice and fresh white fish poached and baked in butter and milk sauce.

Baby carrots with butter, sugar and parsley were a favourite vegetable, adding colour to the plate, and sometimes finely sieved delicious fresh mushroom soup. For dessert her daily favourite was cooked fruit with custard, and a baked egg custard with its smooth texture was a particular treat. Apples and pears seemed to be the easiest for digestion, but my mother also enjoyed apricots and peaches.

Pumpkin and coconut cream soup

Delicious and comforting, this is also colourful. If you choose the grey-skinned variety it will give the soup a good deep-orange colour. It freezes well.

100g butter
1 tbsp oil
1 red onion, chopped finely
2 cloves garlic, crushed
1.2kg pumpkin, peeled, deseeded and cut into small pieces
pepper and salt
500ml chicken stock
500ml water
½ tspn grated nutmeg
1 × 400ml can coconut cream

1 Put the butter and oil in a large heavy-based saucepan.
2 Add the onion and garlic and sauté until clear.
3 Add the pumpkin, pepper and salt and continue to cook, stirring the pumpkin and onion mixture to prevent it from sticking.
4 Add the stock, water and nutmeg and simmer with the lid on until the pumpkin is soft.
5 Remove from the heat and add the coconut cream.
6 Allow to cool and then blend.

SERVES 6

Potato and kumara bake

This is creamy, tasty and deeply comforting.

2–4 potatoes, peeled
1 kumara (red-skinned variety), scrubbed and peeled
125ml cream
pepper and salt
50g butter

1 Preheat the oven to 180°C.
2 Slice the potatoes and kumara into an ovenproof dish, layering and mixing them.
3 Pour the cream over the veges, season with salt and pepper and dot with butter.
4 Bake at 180°C for 30 minutes.

SERVES 2–4

Chicken breast for one

This is simple to do, whether you use coconut cream or orange juice.

1 chicken breast
salt and pepper
120ml coconut cream (optional)
juice of 1 orange (optional)
1 tbspn olive oil
1 sprig thyme

1 Preheat the oven to 160°C.
2 Place the chicken in a small ovenproof dish and season with salt and pepper.
3 Pour in the liquids and olive oil and add the thyme.
4 Cover with tinfoil and bake for 30 minutes.

SERVES 1

White fish poached in butter and milk sauce

Be careful not to overcook the fish, to retain its flavour and soft texture. I like to use terakihi, monkfish or cod for this simple dish.

fillets of white fish
milk
butter
salt and pepper

1 Preheat the oven to 190°C.
2 Place the fish in an ovenproof dish. Pour over enough milk to cover the fish, and dot with butter.
3 Season with salt and pepper and bake for about 15 minutes until the fish looks cooked.

Kumara in orange juice and honey

1 kumara, peeled and cut into small pieces
juice of 1 orange
1 tspn clover honey, heated to liquid
olive oil
salt and pepper

1. Preheat the oven to 180°C.
2. Put the kumara into an ovenproof baking dish.
3. Add the orange juice and honey.
4. Sprinkle with olive oil and season with salt and pepper.
5. Bake for 10 to 20 minutes until the kumara is soft, turning the kumara frequently to keep it moist.

SERVES 2

Mushroom soup

Light and delicious, this recipe allows the full flavour of the mushrooms to come through while retaining the subtle texture. It's a bit fiddly to make but worth the effort. A very nourishing soup, it can be strained for those on a texture-modified diet.

3 tbspn chopped onion
35g butter
3 tbspn flour
1.25 litres heated chicken stock

1 bay leaf
1 sprig of thyme
550g mushrooms
25g butter, extra
juice of 1 lemon
salt and pepper, to taste
150ml cream
2 egg yolks, beaten
finely chopped parsley
fresh nutmeg

1 Cook the onion and butter slowly for 8 to 10 minutes, until tender but not brown.
2 Add the flour, stir in and then add the stock and herbs, stirring well. Continue to heat.
3 Remove the mushroom stems, chop and put into the stock.
4 Bring to the boil and continue simmering for 20 to 30 minutes.
5 Take off the heat and strain the mixture, pressing all the juices through.
6 In another heavy-based small frying pan, gently fry the chopped mushroom caps in the extra butter, adding the lemon juice, salt and pepper.
7 When these have cooked, add the strained stock and continue to heat through.
8 Add the cream and egg yolks and stir well.
9 Bring to the point of simmering until all is heated through.
10 Serve with a sprinkle of parsley and a grind of nutmeg.

SERVES 4–6

Baked egg custard

With poached seasonal fruit, I find this is the ultimate comfort food when I'm feeling fragile.

4 eggs
½ cup caster sugar
300ml milk
300ml cream
1 tspn vanilla essence
freshly grated nutmeg, to sprinkle

1 Preheat the oven to 150°C.
2 Whisk the eggs and sugar together until just combined.
3 Heat the milk, cream and vanilla essence in a saucepan over medium heat until just below boiling point, then remove from the heat and pour over the egg mixture.
4 Beat until just combined, then strain the mixture into a 1-litre baking dish.
5 Sprinkle the surface of the custard with grated nutmeg.
6 Place the dish into a deep roasting pan and fill with enough boiling water to come halfway up the sides of the baking dish.
7 Bake for 45 minutes until just set. Serve warm.

SERVES 4–6

To provide for my mother's modified diet, plastic containers were purchased and mass cook-ups began, followed by hand-processing with a Mouli, just as I had for my young children and grandchildren. Each meal-sized container was labelled, keeping each part of the meal separate inside the pottles. That way my mother still had the pleasure of seeing her meal on the plate with its natural colours. The containers were stored in the freezer and others helped me choose and deliver the food each day. Our mother received comfort from her last meals—they were food she knew and liked. While her desire to eat was diminishing, her memory of good food was not. On her last day, she heard me mention buying fresh scallops the night before.

'I used to love scallops,' she said, looking quite animated. 'Do you think I could have some, dear?'

'Of course you can, Mum.'

'Is it silly of me to ask?' she said. 'You must think I'm crazy asking to eat scallops, but I did love them, especially the way Dale used to cook them on the barbecue.' She was recalling my brother's seafood cook-ups.

'What if you go to all the trouble of getting them and cooking them, and then I can't eat them?'

'Don't worry, Mum, it doesn't matter. We can always eat them if you don't,' I assured her.

At 10 am on the day my mother died, I drove to the fish market near the wharves and collected one dozen scallops, then went back to her house and quickly seared them with a tiny bit of butter, oil and coriander and put them in a crockery dish ready to deliver to Mum in her room in the hospital wing of the retirement village. By now, the staff had become used to all our comings and goings, so no one took any notice.

She saw them, she smelt them and she was excited. 'But how will I eat them, dear?'

'Well, you could suck them or we could mash them up. However you want. Just try a little.'

She took a taste and then looked bewildered. 'It doesn't taste as I remember scallops,' she said. 'I'm sorry dear, I can't eat them.'

The thoughts and memories of the food were there, but she was already leaving us. The delicious seared scallops weren't wasted. They gave my sister and I energy for what lay ahead.

Seared scallops

What a treat, especially when they are fresh from the sea.

1 dozen scallops (fresh or frozen)
butter
coriander leaves, finely chopped (optional)
lemon wedges (optional)

1 Heat a heavy-based frying pan or grill plate to a high heat.
2 Melt a little butter and immediately sear the scallops, turning them at least once.
3 Serve immediately with fresh coriander and lemon wedges, if using.

SERVES 3

CHAPTER 28

En Provence

In September 2008, late summer, I was in the Luberon Valley, Provence, in a cottage with friends. The focus of each day was food—its gathering and preparation—but most important of all was the consuming and the sense of community it brought. This was my first visit back since before my head injury. I was nervous, wondering how I'd manage the journey and the change of environment. Not only did I cope with all the delicious indulgence, I bloomed! Mind you, who wouldn't, with long breakfasts, lunches and dinners when we thought we simply could not eat another thing, but found ourselves sitting down to savour yet another meal?

Occasionally we ventured out to local eateries but on this visit we were disappointed. We weren't sure if the local cooking had deteriorated over the last five or so years, or if our palates and expectations had changed. What worked wonderfully for us, instead, was local produce, coupled with our cooking enthusiasm and a repertoire of dishes accumulated over many years, with the inclusion of a mix of Euro/New Zealand/Pacific style cooking that has come to be known as fusion.

We sat down to gorgeous fresh, highly colourful lunches of tomato salads, the ingredients coming from local tomato grower

Jean Luc's garden, Le Potager d'un Curieux (The Curious Potager).
We'd never seen so many varieties or experienced such tastes, from
luscious red to lime green, yellow and deep-purple varieties—Raison
vert, Poire jeaune, Mirabelle jaune, Cerise noir—to name a few of
the many we used for our colourful chopped tomato lunch salad.

Tomato, mozzarella and basil salad

Stunning to look at and absolutely delicious when prepared using
the perfect produce. Don't attempt this unless you have large, tasty,
fresh tomatoes and a good buffalo mozzarella cheese.

large fleshy red tomatoes
buffalo mozzarella
balsalmic vinegar
fresh basil leaves
black pepper

1 Slice the tomatoes into large rounds.
2 Place on a serving dish.
3 Slice the mozzarella into large rounds.
4 Place one round on top of each of the tomato slices.
5 Sprinkle with a splash of balsamic vinegar and garnish with fresh basil
   leaves.
6 Finally, grind pepper over the finished platter and serve.

Sarah's summer tomato salad

This is fresh and delicious and has eye appeal if you can make it with a mix of brightly coloured tomatoes.

2 cloves garlic
500g small tomatoes
pepper and salt, to taste
balsamic vinegar
olive oil
fresh basil leaves

1 Rub the inside of a salad bowl with the garlic.
2 Cut the tomatoes into quarters and put them in the bowl.
3 Season to taste and splash with vinegar and olive oil.
4 Scatter basil leaves on top.

SERVES 4

Each day we bought a baguette from Christine's Pâtisserie in the nearest village of Saignon, five minutes away by car or a twenty-minute walk. Her pastries were divine, too: tarte au citron, tarte Louis Philipe, tarte Provençale, tarte aux pommes. Accompanied by the local rosé biologique—it's nine euros a bottle and very quaffable. We were very happy. It was perfect—four friends sharing a house, as we had done so many times over the years both in New Zealand and around the world, and each day we purchased fresh food for the day ahead.

On our first night together, dinner was cooked in the tiny, two-storeyed, one-bedroomed house our friends were staying in until the house we would share became available. We arrived after a long drive from Sylvie and Jean-Claude's house in Vallauris, near Nice. It was late afternoon and the sun was a golden orb. The little stone house was set in a lavender field. Our friends Sarah and Philip had prepared thyme-infused lamb with perfect green beans and baby potatoes and a gorgeous richly coloured red pepper salad. (The Provençal lamb does taste different from New Zealand lamb, I think sweeter as if the thyme in the diet has infused the meat!) There were fresh white peaches, blackberries and crème fraîche to follow.

We accompanied the food with local Luberon wines and cheeses, a comté and brie—two of our favourites. What a perfect way to begin a holiday.

Saignon tarte au citron

This recipe allows for one medium-sized tart, but can also be made as smaller individual tarts.

For the pastry
150g butter
1 large egg
75g sugar
250g flour

For the filling
120g butter, softened
200g sugar
zest and juice of 3 juicy lemons
5 eggs, lightly beaten

1 Preheat the oven to 180°C.

2 Make the pastry by processing all the ingredients in a food processor on medium, until a ball of dough forms. This is a very crumbly short pastry. Roll it out to a 34cm circle and line the base and sides of a 26cm loose-bottomed tart tin. Don't worry if the pastry breaks into pieces. Simply press it together in the tin by hand.

3 To make the filling, combine the butter and sugar in a bowl over a saucepan of boiling water and beat until smooth.

4 Grate in the lemon zest and add the juice.

5 Add the eggs and continue beating over the hot water until the mixture begins to thicken.

6 Pour the mixture into the pastry base and bake for 35 to 40 minutes until the filling is set and the base cooked.

7 Cool before removing from the tin.

SERVES 6

Red pepper salad

An intensely colourful and delicious addition to so many meals.

4 large red peppers
balsalmic vinegar
olive oil
salt

1 Preheat the oven to 200°C.

2 Roast the peppers until the skins have charred.

3 Remove the peppers from the oven and put them into a plastic bag to sweat and loosen the skins.

4 Remove the skin and seeds and slice the flesh into large chunks.

5 Put into a serving bowl and sprinkle with balsamic vinegar and olive oil.

6 Season to taste with salt.

SERVES 4–6

With mood elevated by both the setting and our hostess, tanned by the long French summer, dinner the second night seemed all the more flavoursome as Sarah produced a dish from New Zealand that she'd adapted for local ingredients—baked aubergine and tomato topped with parmesan.

Aubergine and parmesan bake

A simple and always appreciated dish, which can be a meal on its own with salad or served as an accompaniment to chicken or meat.

2 aubergine
salt
oil
2 cloves garlic
300g tomato pulp or 2 × 400g cans peeled Roma tomatoes
salt and pepper
1 tspn sugar
freshly grated parmesan

1 Preheat the oven to 170°C.

2 Prepare the aubergines by slicing lengthways and smearing with salt.

3 After 10 to 15 minutes, dry off and fry in batches in the oil in a very hot frying pan or on a grill, browning on both sides.

4 When these have been partially cooked, place them in layers in a baking dish.

5 Mix the garlic and tomato together and season with salt, pepper and a little sugar.

6 Pour the tomato mixture over the eggplant and top with the parmesan. Bake for 30 to 40 minutes.

SERVES 4

Each evening we accompanied our main dish with fresh vegetables and we allowed ourselves larger portions of these than we would be offered in traditional French cuisine, delighting in the crispness of the green beans and the varieties of potato.

For the third night, we bought caille (quail) from the local supermarket and it was my turn to cook. They were dear little fresh plump birds and my friend and I were persuaded to use farce (stuffing) made by the local butcher. It's a mixture of pork, veal and tomato. Looks good and tastes good when cooked and it certainly plumps up the little birds and keeps them moist, but we ate too much, too late in the evening, and a night of indigestion ensued. We decided it was a good idea to stuff the birds, but not such a good idea to stuff ourselves. Cutting off the tiny heads before baking didn't excite one of our diners, but they make the tastiest stock.

The dessert, an attempt to cheat and buy something from the local supermarket, was an absolute failure. It was too sweet and definitely not to be repeated. This isn't to say the supermarket can't provide delicious easy desserts, as it does on other occasions—a perfectly good crème caramel and crème brûlée can be purchased cheaply and the earthenware dishes they come in are great to keep.

Slow-baked quail with thyme, shallots and grapes

You'll have to make your own stock for this—put the heads of the birds in a saucepan with onions, carrots, a bay leaf, a sprig of thyme, some salt and pepper and 2 litres of water. Simmer to reduce for about 30-40 minutes.

4 quail, butterflied
salt and pepper
knob of butter
6–8 shallots
1 medium-sized bunch of green, seedless grapes
2 cloves garlic, crushed
100ml extra virgin olive oil
1/3 cup quail stock

1 Preheat the oven to 180°C.
2 Season the quail with salt and pepper.
3 Heat the butter in a heavy-based frying pan and braise the quail to brown on all sides.
4 Remove the quail and place skin-side up in a cast-iron or heavy-bottomed baking dish.
5 Add the shallots, grapes and garlic, then the olive oil.
6 Pour in the stock, cover the dish with tinfoil and bake for 1 hour until the birds are tender.

SERVES 4

After the quail, we decided to go vegetarian for a couple of days. That was easy in those parts—there was a potato pie (see Potato cheese pie, page 36) and ratatouille on what came to be known as 'burnt jacket' night when a faulty light in our wardrobe installed to provide boudoir ambience almost caused a major fire after I put clothes too close to it. Luckily, we were saved by a leather bag!

We were very excited to find a small biologique (organic) store open on a Sunday, with crates of fresh vegetables from the owner's garden. Those perfect aubergines, small but so tasty, courgettes and red peppers, giant and hot from the sun, with bunches of fresh basil produced an intoxicating meal—the ratatouille smelled divine. We soaked up the last juices with the end of the breakfast baguette accompanied by some local vin rouge. At between six and eight euros a bottle we weren't too worried when we struck a failure and had to abandon a bottle, tipping it down the drain. We were due a failure and on the sixth night the chicken dish went horribly wrong, but I was too tired to care.

The days moved on in a delightful blur. There were shopping expeditions, village visits and forest walks, but the rhythm of the day continued to focus on food—its purchase, preparation and ingestion. We had lamb again, marinated in herbs from our potager and barbecued. It was superb.

I decided to try to do a fillet of beef. At the supermarket Mark and I headed towards the charcuterie section. We'll recognise the cut, I assured him, and we did, although it can be very confusing in French supermarkets as some of the meat cuts are very different from New Zealand cuts. Lots of things were still confusing and a source of both frustration and amusing events as we wove our way through the days.

Something as simple as trying to clean the kitchen sink could turn into a major problem as I puzzled over the large number of cleaning liquids under the sink. I chose one and sprayed—it seemed to do the job, the sink looked cleaner, but my arms and hands were stinging. After a few days of using it to clean sinks and baths, I put my glasses on and discovered it was oven cleaner and a very powerful one at that.

The sky in Luberon was difficult to believe, so clear and star filled. It brought a sense of awe, and a calming peace, as I related to this beautiful landscape. It really is one of the most perfect places I know at this season. And with a swimming pool at our disposal, we could cope with even the hottest days. We watched the sun set over the valley, first bright red then pink. We stood and watched it slip away, leaving us another velvety perfect evening ahead.

Friday, 29 August was another day in paradise for us and a momentous one for democrats in the US with the acceptance speech from Barack Obama for the nomination for the US presidency. We sat and watched it on SKY TV in our little sitting room in Saignon, on one of the rare occasions when our TV was working. It gave us a renewed sense of hope for a change in world politics.

That night there was a first on the food front for us—small white-fleshed, fresh fish. It was wonderful. I'd asked a local and she affirmed my choice. 'Yes,' she said, 'bare is excellent, especially if it's wild.'

I felt proud of myself. It's always intimidating in a new country hunting down specific ingredients so our days felt successful when we managed to bring home what we needed for the evening meal. That night we enjoyed Christine's freshly baked tarts for dessert and this time I added some slow-cooked nectarines, baked in fresh orange juice infused with a vanilla bean.

Poached nectarines in fresh orange juice

This a perfectly simple and satisfying way to eat nectarines, bringing out their full flavour.

6–8 nectarines
freshly squeezed juice of 2 oranges
½ cup sugar
½ cup water
sprig of thyme

1 Preheat the oven to 150°C.
2 Halve the nectarines and remove the stones.
3 Put the orange juice, sugar and water in a saucepan and heat until the sugar has dissolved.
4 Place the nectarines in a baking dish and pour the syrup over the fruit.
5 Place a sprig of thyme on top and bake for about 1 hour.
6 Cover the nectarines and leave to marinate in the syrup for a few hours.

SERVES 4

The next night we decided to risk going out to a local restaurant as we would be relocating to a new cottage, and I hoped it would be as good. Outside, the crickets were making their cricket noises and a gentle breeze wafted in through the open window. All my worries seemed to float away in this incredible, gentle place. I felt slightly embarrassed by our focus on food, but also extremely content.

It was Monday, 1 September. I'd just come to lie down and rest after yet another delightful French lunch, sitting in dappled sunlight under the wisteria-covered terrace, supping on chilled rosé and dishes made with Jean-Luc's delicious tomatoes. It was not quite as hot as it had been, thank goodness, and I was beginning to master the shutters on the doors and windows, having learnt their value in blocking unwanted sunlight in the middle of the day.

Lunch was welcome indeed after I found myself the focus of a Frenchman's rage, when he spotted me asleep in the driver's seat of our car three-quarters of the way up a mountain road—Forest de Vie. He was almost speechless with anger at finding me there. Mark had gone for a walk for at least half an hour and, as I can no longer walk far, I had curled up in the car for a rest. I knew the road was rough and we certainly hadn't seen any other cars there. Mark had wanted to get me and my walking stick to a part of the terrain otherwise inaccessible to me. I was persuaded, just, and didn't read the signs banning public vehicles.

The forest ranger had obviously been alerted to our presence on the mountain and arrived at great speed in his small green van. He was hot and bothered because it was almost midday and he had to eat. He was hungry and frustrated at this dumb woman in her car on the mountain.

My French became even more minimal in the circumstances. He hung around, trying to bully me into going right away, leaving Mark to walk down the mountain. Tell him, tell him, he demanded in rapid French. I pleaded ignorance until finally he checked with his superior by telephone. He asked me to promise we would leave as soon as my husband returned. I gave my promise.

He jumped in his van, eager to leave, his obligation over. As he left I said, 'Mon mari c'est un forestière en Nouvelle Zealande.' (My husband is a forester in New Zealand.) He relaxed, then smiled. 'Eh bien,' he beamed, and drove off down the mountain.

Mark continued to negotiate the food purchasing on his own, with minimal French, but a determination to fulfil the list he was given as well as he could. I had found some ancient cookbooks in the house the night before and set my sights on poussin (small baby chicken) for dinner. He came back with four small birds, but they were quail again. No matter, they were easily adapted to the recipe.

Dessert that night was slow-poached peaches served with crème fraîche. We all agreed this was the best holiday ever, doing all the cooking for ourselves, especially when the other cook was our friend Sarah. The red wine we recommend is from the vineyard Constantin-Chevalier—Côte du Luberon 2004, very smooth and rich.

Poached peaches with vanilla

A delicately flavoured version of poached peach which reminds me of Saignon.

½ cup sugar
2 cups water
2 fresh basil leaves
6 white-fleshed peaches
1 vanilla bean

1 Preheat the oven to 140°C.
2 Put the sugar, water and basil in a saucepan and heat until the sugar has dissolved. Set aside until the basil has infused the syrup.

3 Peel the peaches and put them in a baking dish whole if small and halved if large. Strain the syrup over the peeled peaches and place the vanilla bean in the liquid. Cover the dish.

4 Bake for up to 1 hour, depending on the size of the peaches.

SERVES 4

During our visit we had the feeling that maybe the good cooks and connoisseurs ate at home in Provence. When you're living in the heart of the Luberon and you have to drive between 25 and 50 minutes to find a quality restaurant, something very strange is going on. Either our food sensibilities had increased and our standards were higher or the quality of local restaurants had dropped. Sadly, I think the latter was true and I'm not sure why. Perhaps some of the older restaurants and traditions are dying off. Perhaps there have been too many tourists and standards have been allowed to drop unquestioned, or perhaps the local produce is just so fantastic, and the pace of life so slow, that people celebrate in their own kitchens and enjoy good food at home. If the aromas wafting from open windows, the long lunch hours and the amount of produce purchased at the markets were any indication I believed my hypothesis had some credibility. Whatever was happening, we still thought it was absolutely wonderful the way food and living were celebrated there, where these villages maintained the rhythm of life passed down over centuries.

The lavender fields, harvested, rested quietly. They had autumn and a harsh winter to get through before they would bloom again. Our washing flapped in the wind on the long lines, hung between the trees, fresh and clean and dried right through by the warm dry breeze.

My three companions were out walking the gorge where Mark had encountered a huge wild pig that morning. Not known for exaggeration, Mark described the pig as being the size of a small cattle beast, galloping off with thundering hoofs. He had hoped to meet some early boletus ceps after downpours the previous two nights, but not a wild beastie.

On 5 September, our last full day in the north of Provence, I was filled with sunshine and the aromas of fresh herbs. Thyme, rosemary and lavender hangs in the air. They grow wild underfoot so that with every step there was that deeply satisfying perfume conveying memories of wonderful meals shared with friends.

CHAPTER 29

Going gastronomique

After weeks of cooking for ourselves I thought it was time to treat ourselves to a true French gastronomique experience—not in Paris, where it would be outrageously expensive, but somewhere en route to Paris. The journey to l'Abbaye de la Bussière, secluded in the Burgundy countryside, was memorable and arduous, largely due to extreme weather conditions in the north of the Rhone Valley. Since my injury, I didn't do car journeys particularly well. Unfortunately, we also found ourselves in bumper-to-bumper traffic and a journey that should have taken 5 to 6 hours took us 12 hours. At one point on the A7, the four- or five-lane main road was stacked up for 58 kilometres. Surprisingly, people were very well behaved. We travelled 80 kilometres over five hours and sometimes were at a complete stop for 5 to 10 minutes. It was amazing to see how people coped with this situation and the normal anonymity of car travel was turned on its head as we got out and attempted to communicate in all our different languages.

I was approached by a young man whose car was directly behind us in lane two. He was from Algeria and had been driving his family, his wife and three children, for three days, and now this. 'C'est pas normalement?' he asked. While post-holiday French traffic is notoriously bad, the cause this time was severe flooding in the north. So no, it was certainly not normal!

His three little children, a boy and two girls, were very patient. I asked them if they would like some chocolate and they looked so excited. I couldn't get it to them at that point because the traffic began to move, but at the next stop I managed to pass a pain au raisin (small raisin bread) and the chocolate through their car window. It was so fast I was unable to see their little faces, but heard their exclamation. 'Merci, merci!' I was pleased to be able to give them a tiny bit of pleasure on their long journey. After all, meeting their little family had certainly given me pleasure.

At 11 pm we finally made it to the l'Abbaye. The beauty of the grounds and the region itself, with a delightful little village and a large picture-book medieval castle overlooking the verdant landscape below, met all expectations. Everything looked green and lush and it was cool. We dropped from temperatures in the thirties in the south to around between 14 and 18 degrees.

The chef, Olivier, an absolutely delightful and unassuming young man from the Alsace, had a real passion and love for food, which showed in his menus. Everything was in perfect combination. The décor of the dining rooms was breathtaking in its quiet beauty. We wouldn't say the same about some of the renovations to the bedrooms, which in our opinion seemed overdone.

We breakfasted simply each day but on the second night treated ourselves to the full works, dining gastronomique. We were not disappointed. We began by choosing the menu de l'Abbaye, which at 60 euros turned out to be a superb choice and relatively inexpensive compared to what we would pay in New Zealand at a top restaurant. The appetiser arrived—shrimp in the lightest of batters and another morsel I couldn't easily identify, but it was delicious, accompanied by bread and roasted dried slithers of beetroot, potato and sweet potato.

This was followed by an entrée. For me, Olivier created some mackerel and herbs, crisp and light. For Mark a cep mousse presented in a shot glass, which he pronounced delicious. Next the escargot for me, and for Mark foie gras and fig.

The escargot was an unforgettable mastery and fusion of art and cuisine. It arrived on a high board covered in fake grass, looking like a lawn. A long white plate sat on the grass, setting off the dish to perfection. A single snail in its shell—the traditional presentation—was accompanied by at least five or six others, hidden in a light creamy sauce captured by a choux pastry. They were all very hot. Perfect.

We then both had salmon and I've never tasted such light and delicious salmon, presented as a very small, perfectly rectangular piece with lightly crisped skin.

The next course was the main. For me the female duck (canette) and for Mark the classic boeuf à la Bourguignon, with a modern twist. I thought back to my first encounter with the French classic in the 1970s, and see this—the creation of a top chef almost 40 years later. The tastes were intensified by the reduction of juices and the meat was presented to perfection, not lost in the sauce; it was separate from it.

As for my duck . . . well, let me just say that in all my attempts to eat duck over the years, this was the very best. Tender yet firm, skin slightly coloured but not crisp, a small perfect portion and a jus of such delicious qualities accompanied by the finest lattice work potato rounds—it was a masterpiece both to look at and to taste.

We moved on to the cheese course, having already seen the most amazing selection of cheeses wheeled in to other tables. Magnificent rounds of cheeses were cut to perfection then covered in what I was told was a traditional woven basket, like an upside-down baby's bassinette, lined with fine mesh for keeping insects off the cheese—they were both functional and beautiful.

Our cheese came with a difference. An époisses de Bourgogne, a local speciality, is served hot and dripping with sweet nuttiness, surrounded by light puff pastry. It simply melted into your mouth. We were now ready for dessert and the meal had been so beautifully balanced we didn't feel full.

Dessert arrived—a sablé biscuit with raspberries in a crème, with a sculptured circle of brandy snap on top and to the side. Sitting perfectly balanced at the base of the circle was an oval-shaped almond ice cream. After that, which was divine, we thought we could go no further when one last offering was made—sweet treats including a chocolate truffle of exceptional quality.

And then a coffee and a tea upstairs in a sitting room of our choice and a visit from the chef.

I felt very privileged indeed. We left l'Abbaye de la Bussière understanding why it had earned *Harper's Bazaar* magazine's Best Hide Away of the Year for 2008. It fully deserves its international accolades.

Fromage chaud

The cheese will be very runny, so it can be messy, but no one minds as it is so delicious.

Serve with either a dessert wine or a muscat, or it goes equally well with pinot noir or syrah. We often ate this before the dessert course in France and it's been a great hit at home in Christchurch.

I purchase my époisses de Bourgogne, beautiful in its wooden box, from Martin at Canterbury Cheesemongers, who tells me how to prepare it.

1 young époisses de Bourgogne
¼ cup white wine, chardonnay or pinot gris

1 Preheat the oven to 180°C.
2 Remove the plastic wrapper from the cheese and replace the cheese in the box.
3 Prick the surface of the cheese in a number of places and then sprinkle with white wine.
4 Place the wooden lid back on the cheese and put it in another baking dish in case it leaks as the cheese heats up.
5 Place the cheese in the oven just before you're ready to serve and heat for 15 to 20 minutes.
6 Take from the oven, remove the wooden box and serve with pieces of fresh warmed baguette.

CHAPTER 30

Return to Paris

Over twenty years and many visits, I had almost always stayed down the hill around St Michel, frequenting Rue Saint-André-des-Arts and its surrounds. This time, over the last clamorous two days, I decided the noise levels had reached my limit. The charm of Hotel Saint-André-des-Arts, which had satisfied many of my acquaintances and family over the years with its quirky staff and even quirkier accommodation, had lost its appeal. In recent years Rue Saint-André-des-Arts had gained a noisy bar and an internet café that opened almost around the clock. The racket went on well into the small hours and although closing the windows quelled the noise, the late summer heat made sleep elusive. It was either air and a cooling breeze and a racket and a waft of a malfunctioning sewerage system, or overwhelming heat and some quiet.

On a previous visit I had both air, quiet and views when I was given the very top suite on the fifth floor. You wouldn't want to be tall or have weight or health issues though, as the climb up was extreme, there being no lift in the rambling, ancient establishment. The roof, however, had been upgraded and now had windows that could be opened, and provided glorious views across the rooftops of Paris.

I had enjoyed some wonderful times here over the years and the proprietor, Henri, guided me to some of the best concerts, music stores and eating places in Paris—returning to the same hotel was worth it because I felt as if I had to do an apprenticeship before Henri finally gave me some of the addresses. At last, after many hit and miss attempts, I was able to fulfil my dream of experiencing simple food cooked the way I'd read about.

But now it was 2008, and my tolerance for noise and bustle had diminished. I sat on the computer searching for almost two days to find another hotel with charm, within budget, and within the area I had come to know and love between Quartier Saint-Germain-des-Prés, the Sorbonne and Boulevard Saint-Michel. This small but heavenly area held so many pleasurable things—food, fashion, antiquuities, music and beautiful gardens. For me, memories of Paris were all here and I loved it all: the vast, expansive, inspiring Luxembourg Gardens, the fashionable streets around Saint-Germain-des-Prés, the gorgeousness of the architecture on the Île de la Cité, with Sainte-Chapelle, Notre-Dame, the Tuilleries and concerts. The wonderful food is still there, if you do your homework.

We shifted up the hill, nearer to the Sorbonne, next door to the Théâtre de l'Odéon and just two minutes from the Luxembourg Gardens. Food was uppermost on my mind as we settled into the Hotel Jardin de L'Odeon, which was clean, with original décor and quiet. Our limits were distance from the hotel and budget, and we were purely interested in French fare, away from places frequented by tourists. As always, I wanted to find the genuine places owned and loved by French people who were still proud of producing classic dishes.

That's no small ask in Paris. Even back in 1939, writer and gourmand A J Liebling commented on his return in the fall, 'After an absence of 12 years, I noticed a decline in the serious quality of restaurants that could not be blamed on the war.' He writes: 'The food of France, although it has gone off disastrously, is still the best there is.' Of the Michelin guide which emerged in the 1930s,

Liebling comments: 'It ominously began to be the arbiter of where to dine, so this was the beginning of large numbers of the travelling public, now motorised, lunching in a hurry resulting in small town hotels, small towns themselves beginning to die.' I read on, surprised by how early the decline is reported to have begun—well before I was born—let alone conscious of the delights of eating.

I decided it was all relative—while Liebling has his heaven in pre-1939 Paris, I had mine sixty years later. In 1999, I was in heaven at the delights French cuisine could offer the poor but discerning visitor, at a very reasonable price.

In 2008, seventy years after Liebling's disappointment and twenty years after my first visit, I have finally encountered a similar sense of loss. Even armed with knowledge from previous visits, and despite the best of guidance from well-respected café guides and the recommendations of locals, we still had disappointing, difficult and expensive eating experiences. Paris, as always, is busy, so bookings were required for restaurants, especially at more sought-after venues.

The Michelin guide to quality restaurants of Paris was obviously doing the job well, but as I commented to one of the waiters, I hadn't travelled all the way to Paris to have two garrulous English-speaking diners loudly discussing politics just a metre away at the next table. Politics featured hugely on this journey, with international financial markets in turmoil. Some days, the future looked very bleak, so it was with a degree of anger I found myself trying to stay calm, as I juggled between ordering my escargots and veal, and unavoidably eavesdropping on their loud conversation.

After a few mouthfuls of escargot and the effort required to use the implement to hold them steady was mastered, we were sufficiently distracted to take in the ambience and food. Of course, no meal would be complete without dessert and this time it was a superb crème brûlée with pears baked in red wine.

Crème brûlée

After eating this classic in many countries over many years, I decided to try my hand at making my own. This is a simple and reliable recipe.

500ml cream
500ml milk
1 tspn vanilla essence or 1 vanilla bean split
*   lengthways*
6 egg yolks
140g sugar

1 Combine the cream, milk and vanilla bean, if using, in a large heavy-based saucepan and bring to simmering point but do not boil.
2 Whisk the egg yolks and sugar together until thick and pale, then gradually pour the mixture into the heated milk and cream.
3 Stir in the vanilla essence.
4 Continue cooking for about 30 minutes, stirring constantly, until the mixture starts to thicken.
5 Let the mixture sit for 5 minutes, then pour the custard into 8 shallow ramekins.
6 Cool and refrigerate for at least 3 hours, or overnight.
7 When ready to serve, sprinkle with sugar, then brown the sugar with a cook's torch or place the ramekins under a hot grill for a very short time, but you need to keep the custard cold in order to caramelise the sugar.
8 Serve immediately.

SERVES 8

Pears baked in red wine

An adaptation of this, which is equally delicious, uses white wine and honey in place of the red wine and sugar, and in that case I add sprigs of thyme and grated lemon zest when the pears are cooking.

6 pears
120g sugar
1 stick of cinnamon
1 bottle red wine
grated zest of 1 orange
2 cloves

1 Preheat the oven to 150°C.
2 Peel the pears carefully, leaving them whole with the stalk intact.
3 Arrange the pears in a deep oven-proof dish.
4 Make a syrup by heating all the other ingredients together until the sugar is dissolved.
5 Pour the syrup over the pears—they should be covered by the syrup.
6 Cover the dish with a casserole lid or tin foil.
7 Bake for 1 to 3 hours, depending on the variety of pear.
8 Turn the pears from time to time.
9 Serve warm or cold.

SERVES 6

A highlight of this visit was a picnic with my niece in the Luxembourg Gardens. I love going to the local markets in Saint-Germain and choosing the ingredients from the street stalls—fresh fruit, peaches, melon, raspberries, pastries, baguettes, saucisson and cheese. We sat under the avenue of lime trees on the bench seats and delighted in the delicious treats in our baskets. The flowering beds were full of dahlias, yellow daisies and cosmos, and the hot sun was muted, filtered by the large lime tree. Hundreds of other lunching Parisians were also enjoying their meals, from a sandwich through to a full picnic. It was a beautiful way to spend the middle of the day in central Paris.

As another journey draws to an end, I'm left thinking about how increasingly difficult it's becoming to find the quality I have been used to—it is more and more elusive. I decide it's the perfection of moments when the uniqueness and adrenaline of a new experience live up to expectation—when the experience, and all the effort you put into it, delivers something satisfying, something perfect.

Whatever it be, a meal, a view from a hotel window, a visit to an acclaimed monument, the people you meet in a new environment or new depths you find in a relationship of many years, it certainly takes more effort as the world becomes busier. The demands on resources increase, the options of what to do and where to go are simply dazzling, and sifting through it all to find precious moments of perfection is becoming more difficult. Those elusive moments are a true rarity, to be treasured.

CHAPTER 31

Keeping it simple

It was November 2008 and six weeks since we had returned from our idyllic vacation in the Luberon. The realities of maintaining 'the good life' were increasingly challenging as the demands of everyday life intruded from every direction. No sooner was one part of the garden weeded than another was out of control and just when it all looked perfect and you felt you could relax, wine in hand, heading out for an early evening catch-up with your husband, you were blasted by winds from the south. Out of nowhere clouds rolled in and the sea raged, white tops showing as the trees began to bend. If it wasn't a southerly, it was a cold easterly. All the gorgeous food had to be shifted inside.

And, of course, being in Canterbury the raging northwesterly really got us going. Trees bend almost double as it raged through. But we're of tough stock, and didn't give up easily and continue planning outdoor events—sometimes we're lucky.

I was preparing a very special dinner for seven old and dear friends, who were gathering to celebrate our friend Sarah's sixtieth birthday. Usually very disciplined, I felt overwhelmed by recent crises in our business, with global financial markets in freefall. Added to this was the shock of returning from a delicious and restful holiday—I just couldn't get myself moving. There were three courses to prepare, shopping to do, a table to set and flowers to be arranged. With house guests as well, my legs turned to lead. How could I possibly do it all without falling apart? I was already feeling fully stretched and I hadn't even set the table!

Here's the answer. When all else turns to custard, set the table, clean up the house, put flowers in the vases, clear the kitchen, empty the dishwasher and start on your list. My close friend and cooking mate Sarah always says, 'Keep it simple, we'll just keep it simple tonight' and I nodded. Remembering her perfect simple meals, I also remembered how challenging it can be to keep everything simple!

Shopping for simple but perfect ingredients is a time-consuming exercise. Hot-smoked salmon from the fishmonger, fresh baguettes from the cheesemonger and the cheeses—all viewed and tasted before purchase. These imported gems were supplemented by local cheeses fresh from the weekend market. Chilled French champagne provided a simple beginning to the meal. For a friend whose wonderful food had been treasured for the past thirty years, it was a fitting gift.

The old advice remains the best—choose a recipe you know well. With no vegetarians on the guest list, I chose an eye fillet of beef in tamari ginger and coriander sauce (see page 178). It works as long as there is some good tamari sauce in the pantry and fresh coriander in my herb pots outside the kitchen door. I had a big chunk of fresh ginger, some garlic, a couple of limes and some good olive oil on hand. Just the eye fillet to order.

I always feel safer when the main is underway, the vegetables prepared and the entrée and hors d'oeuvres sorted. Almonds roasted with rosemary and salted, for nibbles learnt from friends Sarah and Kamila, and a simple, delicious tapenade, then a smoked salmon and baby leek salad for entrée.

Roasted salted almonds

You can add some more salt and rosemary at the time of serving.

150–200g almonds, skins on
tamari sauce
Maldon salt
fresh rosemary, chopped

1 Preheat the oven to 160°C. Line a baking dish with baking paper.
2 Scatter the almonds in a prepared baking dish and bake for 10 to 15 minutes.
3 Remove from the oven and sprinkle liberally with the tamari sauce, salt and rosemary. Shake to coat well.
4 Return to the oven for another 5 minutes.
5 Allow to cool and serve.

Hot-smoked salmon with baby leeks

This is an easy-to-make fresh tasting entrée.

24 baby leeks or 3 or 4 larger leeks, cleaned and cut into 2–3cm lengths
salt and pepper
2 tbspn olive oil
juice of 1 orange
400g hot-smoked salmon
100g snow peas, blanched
½ cup peas, fresh or frozen, cooked

1 fennel bulb, finely sliced (optional)
3 tbspn pitted olives, finely chopped
3 tbspn extra virgin olive oil
3 tbspn lemon juice
1 cup chervil or parsley leaves, stalks removed, finely chopped

1 Preheat the oven to 180°C.
2 Place the leeks in a baking dish that has a lid.
3 Season with salt and pepper and pour the olive oil and orange juice over the leeks.
4 Bake for 30 minutes or until soft.
5 Meanwhile, arrange the salmon, snow peas, peas, sliced fennel and olives on a serving platter or on 8 individual plates.
6 Make a dressing with the extra virgin olive oil and lemon juice.
7 Take the cooled baby leeks and divide them onto the plates or platter and drizzle the dressing over the salad and finish with the fresh herb.

SERVES 8

A great tapenade

This stores well in airtight containers in the refrigerator and, in a pretty jar, makes a wonderful gift for friends.

220g black olives, pitted
3 tbspn capers
6 anchovy fillets
1 clove garlic, crushed
150ml olive oil
1 tbspn lemon juice

2 tspn Dijon mustard
1 tspn chopped thyme
1 tspn chopped parsley

1 Put all the ingredients in a food processor and process until desired texture.

For me, it isn't a special celebration without something sweet—without dessert a dinner just feels wrong. Determined to keep this gathering simple and free of stress, I had frozen a lemon cake for dessert that I made as 'distress therapy' earlier in the week. All that was left to do on the day was to hull the strawberries and soak them in heated grape jelly—it brings out the most delicious flavours—beat the cream, defrost the lemon cake slowly in the oven while the guests were arriving, then assemble between the main and dessert.

Warm lemon cake with strawberries in grape jelly

1 × Fresh lemon cake (see page 182)

For the strawberries in grape jelly
2 punnets strawberries, hulled and cut into small pieces
2–3 tbspn grape jelly (see page 206)
juice of 1 orange

1 For the strawberries, put everything in a bowl and toss lightly, avoiding damaging the strawberries. Set aside to marinate for 2 to 3 hours.
2 When serving, place slices of the warm lemon cake on each serving plate and add this beautiful colourful accompaniment on the side.

By the time we'd finished dessert and the delicious dessert wine that accompanied it, supped tea and coffee and nibbled chocolate-coated ginger pieces, and members of the party were rolling around in various states of sated pleasure, I think I could safely conclude a very successful celebration had been enjoyed with the minimum of fuss.

It all looked simple and we all agreed, simple is best.

I mull this over as we clean up the next day. An empty fridge and mountains of dishes. Simple still seems to equal a lot of effort and expense, but we reassure ourselves how inexpensive it is when you compare eating food of that quality at home to going out to a high-end restaurant.

CHAPTER 32

It's nearly Christmas

It's a looney time of year and pressure mounts for whoever takes on the mountainous task of planning and preparation, with all the present buying and wrapping, writing letters and cards, and keeping everybody happy. It doesn't matter how many times you say 'It'll be different this year . . I'm not going through that stress again,' if you stay at home during December you find yourself on the same old merry-go-round you can't get off.

On 14 December the house was filled with the delicious aroma of a freshly baked Christmas cake—four hours of baking had warmed the house with enticing smells. I used an adaptation of an old family recipe, which has been a much-loved and much-eaten cake over the decades, unfortunately by Labrador dogs, too! My daughter's golden girl, Bella, disgraced herself when she was left alone to guard the wedding gifts. The wedding cake had been neatly cut into pieces and wrapped in foil, as was the custom. Bella's nose for fruit cake drew her to the bench, where she could just reach by standing on her back legs. We came home to empty wrappers and a bloated dog. And this happened not once, but twice, after my sister's wedding also. No one learned a thing from the first time.

Gran and Rosie's Christmas cake

This cake has also been a hit for family weddings. I like to include dried cranberries, candied lemon and orange peel and cherries. It can be made up to three weeks ahead. When cooled, wrap it in tinfoil and newspaper and store in a cool pantry cupboard, where it will stay moist. Once you have cut it, if you wish to use some later, wrap it in tinfoil and store in the freezer. These little parcels from the freezer give much delight for weeks.

500g butter
500g sugar
9 eggs
750g flour
½ tspn cinnamon
½ tspn spice
½ tspn nutmeg
2kg dried fruit
1 tbspn redcurrant jelly
zest and juice of 1 lemon
zest and juice of 1 orange
1/2 tspn vanilla essence
1/2 cup brandy
blanched almonds for decoration instead of icing (optional)

1 Cream the butter and sugar.
2 Beat in the eggs.
3 Add the sifted flour and spices and mix to combine.
4 Add the dried fruit and redcurrant jelly.
5 Add lemon and orange zest and juice and mix to combine.

6 Finally, add the vanilla and brandy and mix to combine.

7 When everything is thoroughly mixed together, cover the bowl and leave to stand overnight.

8 Preheat the oven to 180°C. Line a 26cm diameter (or square) cake tin with baking paper, taking the baking paper lining as high again as the sides of the tin.

9 Spoon the batter into the prepared tin.

10 Arrange the blanched almonds on the surface of the batter, if using, and cover with baking paper.

11 Bake for 1 hour. Remove the cover, return the cake to the oven and lower the oven temperature to 140°C (if possible, turn off the top element). Bake for a further 2 to 2½ hours or longer until a skewer comes out clean.

As is so often the case in Canterbury in early summer, we were having erratic weather—extreme heat with a rapid change to cold as wind lowered the temperature. The image of a South Seas island lifestyle in baking summer heat with people around a barbecue and an outdoor Christmas table is often not what happens. It can be very cool and sometimes wet. Somehow we've combined some of the customs of the festive season we inherited from the northern hemisphere with our own brand that has evolved over many years with variations, depending on whether we're home for Christmas or at a bach.

By 23 December 2010, there were no big commitments left except to cook on Christmas Day. The previous night was a practice run, and was followed the next morning by a delightful feeling I get the morning after a dinner has gone well. As is often the case, it was a pre-Christmas dinner for family members who were travelling and wouldn't be there on Christmas Day. It seemed a bit of a cheat really, managing to squeeze more than one celebration from the same event.

In the southern hemisphere Christmas Day is one of the longest days of the year and twilight here in Canterbury lasts until 10 o'clock. Even in the busyness of the run up to Christmas Day, it was unthinkable to leave fruit to ruin on the bushes so, somehow, we fit in picking and preparing berries—blackcurrants were tailed and gooseberries prepared and turned into delicious tarts.

Fruit mince tarts

There is one tradition that never never varies—that's Christmas fruit mince tarts. The filling can be made up to three months ahead and stored in the fridge ready to make a fuss-free batch of fruit mince tarts during the festive season.

1 batch Sweet short pastry (see page 55)

For the fruit mince
1 cup sultanas
1 cup dried mixed fruit
¾ cup currants
1 medium Granny Smith apple, peeled and grated
finely grated rind of 1 lemon
finely grated rind of 1 orange
1 tbspn lemon juice
½ cup dark brown sugar
¼ cup brandy
1 tspn ground cinnamon
½ tspn ground mixed spice

½ tspn ground nutmeg
½ tspn ground cloves
icing sugar

1 To make the fruit mince, put sultanas, mixed fruit, currants, apple, lemon and orange rinds and juice into a food processor and pulse until finely chopped.
2 Transfer to a bowl.
3 Add the sugar, brandy and spices and stir until well combined.
4 Spoon the fruit mixture into a 2½-cup capacity sterilised screw-top jar and store in the fridge until required.
5 To make a batch of tarts, preheat the oven to 180°C. Grease a 24-cup tartlet tin.
6 Roll the pastry out between two sheets of baking paper until 5mm thick.
7 Using a 7cm-round biscuit cutter, cut 24 rounds from the pastry and line the cups of the tartlet tin.
8 Spoon 1 tbspn of fruit mince into each shell.
9 From the remaining pastry cut 24 small stars and place a star onto the fruit mince mixture in each cup.
10 Bake for 15 to 20 minutes until lightly golden and the pastry is cooked through.
11 Transfer to a wire rack to cool.
12 Dust with icing sugar to serve.

MAKES ENOUGH FOR 36 TARTLETS

For us, Christmas is reasonably traditional, although I've been known to do away with the turkey and ham and settle, instead, for tender, flavoursome, organic chicken with sage and chestnut stuffing and locally reared organic pork racks baked in home-made grape juice and apples. If we're lucky, dessert is black cherries from our tree with a parfait followed by chocolate truffles.

Christmas parfait with marinated cherries

The beauty of this is that it has to be made the day before Christmas.

For the parfait
150g sugar
100ml cold water
6 egg yolks
100g chocolate, chopped
3 tbspn dark rum or Kirsch
2 tspn cinnamon
½ tspn ground cloves
150g fresh cherries, pitted
450ml cream

For the cherries
1kg fresh cherries, pitted
4 tbspn sugar
4 tbspn water
2 tbspn Kirsch

1 To make the parfait, put the sugar and water in a heavy-based saucepan and bring to the boil, stirring to dissolve the sugar. Continue boiling to make a dense syrup.

2 In a bowl, beat the egg yolks until fluffy.
3 While still beating, add the warm sugar syrup and keep beating until the mixture is a pale cream colour and has doubled in volume.
4 At this stage add the chocolate, rum or Kirsch, cinnamon, cloves and cherries.
5 Lastly, fold in the lightly whipped cream.
6 Spoon into a mould and place in the freezer overnight. (I like to use a deep rectangular dish or a loaf tin lined with plastic wrap.)
7 Gently poach the cherries in the sugar and water and lastly add the Kirsch. Store in the fridge in a covered container until required.
8 Serve thick slices of parfait with poached cherries on the side.

SERVES 8–10

Fruity chocolate truffles

The Christmas fruit mince gives these truffles festive flair.

200g dark chocolate
¼ cup cream
1 tbspn dark rum
¼ cup Christmas fruit mince (see page 257)
375 dark chocolate, extra

1 To make the filling, melt the chocolate and cream in a bowl over a saucepan of boiling water.
2 Add the rum and fruit mince and stir to combine. Remove from the heat and set aside to cool and thicken.
3 As soon as possible, roll the mixture into balls. (Don't make them too big—it's a rich mixture.)

4 Refrigerate for at least 4 hours or overnight.

5 Melt the extra chocolate in a bowl over a saucepan of boiling water. Stir until smooth and glossy and remove from the heat to cool but not set.

6 Using a skewer, dip the chilled truffles into the melted chocolate and turn carefully to coat them evenly.

7 Store in the fridge until required.

MAKES 30

And then post-Christmas there's the unwind, using up leftovers, visitors—some unexpected—and trips to the beach, sailing, more cherries and long lunches redolent of France. And for us in Canterbury, we feel as if we're in heaven despite the earthquakes.

It's 28 December. 'Stay on track, a new venture will be successful.' I am urged on by the wisdom in the fortune cookie chocolate I unwrapped after lunch. Never mind the waistline, which has definitely increased in recent months, the taste was as delicious as the scene around me at a table outside the garden house, with an umbrella for shade, a lush lemon tree laden with fruit and teepees of flowering runner beans with their scarlet plumes reaching for the sky providing the backdrop.

The scent of deep-blue velvet petunias and the happy brightness of red geraniums, temperature in the mid-20s and the scene was set for a post-Christmas pre-New Year lunch. Salad with gently fried pieces of leftover ham, chopped hard-boiled free-range eggs collected that morning from the hen house, small organic tomatoes from the market in Lyttelton, and a lettuce straight from the kitchen garden. A lavish assortment of fresh herbs from the garden—basil, parsley, chives, mint—all brought the freshness of summer to the table. The ingredients were tossed and dressed with home-made vinaigrette, to make a sort of Niçoise salad, and we had a great lunch.

A sort of salade Niçoise

I make this with chives and parsley, but you can use other herbs according to taste and availability. It is a delicious way to eat ham left over from Christmas Day.

2 cups small sweet quartered tomatoes
1 cos lettuce, washed and dried
100g pitted black olives
3 hard-boiled eggs, peeled and quartered
6–12 anchovy fillets, pulled into smaller pieces (optional)
2–3 tbspn chopped fresh green herbs
4–5 thick slices ham off the bone, cut into bite-sized pieces and fried
cubes of bread, fried in the pan juices left by the ham

vinaigrette (see page 12)

1 Assemble all the salad ingredients in a bowl or on serving plates, dress with vinaigrette and serve immediately.

SERVES 6–8

After lunch, we relaxed listening to the bees buzzing and the sheep calling to each other on the distant hillside and the birds singing in the garden—a time to dream and rest and be pleased to be here at the bottom of the world in summer. And the Christmas rush over for another year.

CHAPTER 34

Fruit de la mer

In the last week of the long school holidays the greyness finally lifted and the heat and clarity of light we are so well known for arrived at last. We were lucky enough to have our family join us for our annual booking at a tiny isolated beach on Banks Peninsula. The highlight of the family get together lunch was fresh paua prised from the rocks right in front of the house during low tide that morning.

I've had many experiences eating paua, but this has to be the best. Outside the bach there is a huge slab of wood for the outdoor table. Beyond is the small harbour which, on a good day such as this, sparkles like the interior of a paua shell. The grandchildren were fascinated by these black creatures, still alive in the bucket. They were not happy about the prospect of killing them and a grandson stole one to deliver it back to the rocks. The others were cut from their shells and thinly sliced. Each piece was pounded once or twice with a rock to soften its texture. I adapted a recipe for tuatua—it proved to be an immense success.

Grilled paua with lemon tarragon butter

To cook paua you need a really fierce heat, and be prepared to stand over it keeping a watchful eye and constantly turning the pieces of paua. This makes a perfect entrée.

250g butter, coarsely chopped
2 tbspn finely chopped garlic
2–3 tbspn finely chopped fresh tarragon
⅓ cup finely chopped fresh flat-leaf parsley
zest and juice of 2 lemons
2 extra lemons, cut into quarters
freshly ground black pepper
20 medium paua, taken from their shells, washed, dried, pounded and cut
*   into bite-sized pieces*

1 Preheat the barbecue or stovetop grill-plate until hot.
2 Put all the ingredients in a bowl and stir to combine.
3 Cook in batches on a very hot grill and serve as quickly as possible after cooking.

SERVES 6–8 AS AN ENTREE

When the first platter went out to the table the youngest grandchild, then aged three, took a taste. He then took a fork and sat in front of the platter and ate as much as he could with great concentration. An older grandson tentatively took a piece and then exclaimed it was delicious. He said it tasted just like chicken—for him, a good cooked chicken is the benchmark of tasty cuisine.

The challenge had been how to turn out a lunch for ten, with supplies running low. A sausage ragout and a ratatouille with a large platter of pasta with green peas, lemon and pepper and some hot bread fitted the bill. We finished with a mixed fruit salad with whipped cream and yoghurt to follow.

Plum, strawberry and orange fruit salad

This is a beautifully coloured fruit salad.

250g fresh black Doris plums, cut in half, destoned
sugar
2 punnets strawberries, hulled and cut into quarters
2 oranges, peeled, pith removed and cut into small pieces

1 Preheat the oven to 180°C.
2 Put the plums in an ovenproof baking dish and sprinkle with a little sugar.
3 Bake until cooked, then cool before using.
4 Put all the fruit into a serving bowl and mix through so the juices run into each other.
5 Add a little more sugar to taste.

SERVES 6–8

It felt like a rich feast, sitting around the wooden slab covered with a white tablecloth that fluttered in the sea breeze, held down with rocks from the beach. Hot sun, blue sky and the family enjoying each other's company. Perfection.

In Maine I had watched live lobsters dropped into an outdoor boiler turn from dark brown to a bright reddish orange. Back in New Zealand, in Kaikoura, I was given two live crayfish that quietly wriggled in their newspaper wrapping and I felt slightly sick about what I had to do next. I was told by a local fisherman that freezing them briefly will do the deed, so into the freezer in the rental apartment they went. I heard them moving about; it was horrible. Finally they fell silent so into the saucepan of boiling salted water they went. It woke them up and long spiky feelers pressed against the pot lid, pushing it to the floor. I freaked out but kept the heat on them. Then, all was quiet and I took these rigid, shining, bright-orange, amazing dinosaur-beings from the saucepan.

After that description, if anyone is still keen to have a go at making a bouillabaisse or fish stew, here's the recipe I use.

Bouillabaisse Kaikoura

This is my version of the traditional Mediterranean seafood soup. It is rarely the same twice as there are regional variations and it calls for the freshest available fish and shellfish. All the better if you have had a day collecting it yourself!

12 mussels (optional)
12 clams or cockles
500ml white wine

6 large ripe tomatoes
50ml olive oil
1 onion, finely diced
4 cloves garlic, crushed
1 fennel bulb, finely diced
2 sticks celery, finely chopped
sprig of thyme
sprig of parsley
sprig of fennel top
1 tbspn tomato paste
1 piece orange peel
bay leaf
400ml fish stock
2 small crayfish, cooked
2 large green prawns or 12 smaller ones, in the shell
250g each of the following fish: gurnard, snapper, John Dory and monkfish
plain flour
salt
knob of butter
olive oil, extra

1 To prepare the shellfish, remove the beards from the mussels, if using, and wash the shellfish under cold running water to remove any sand.
2 Place a large saucepan over high heat. Add the shellfish and 400ml of the wine.
3 Put the lid on and steam for 3 to 5 minutes until the shells open, shaking the pan often.
4 Do this in batches for all the shellfish, then set aside to cool.
5 Drain and retain the cooking liquid.
6 To prepare the bouillon, peel the tomatoes by plunging first into boiling water for 10 seconds and then into cold. Cut the tomatoes in half, discard the seeds and dice the flesh. Set aside until required.

7 In a heavy-based saucepan, heat the olive oil and sauté the onion, garlic, fennel and celery until soft.

8 Add the herbs and tomato paste and cook for 2 minutes.

9 Add the remaining wine, orange peel and bay leaf and simmer until the liquid has reduced by half.

10 Add the chopped tomato, fish stock and liquid from the mussels. Simmer for a few more minutes, correcting the seasoning, and then allow to cool.

11 Remove the flesh from the crayfish and add it to the saucepan.

12 Add the prawns.

13 Cut the fish fillets into bite-sized pieces and dust with flour seasoned with salt.

14 Heat the butter with the extra olive oil in a heavy-based frying pan and quickly fry the fish pieces. Set aside until required.

15 Add all the seafood to the bouillon base and simmer for a few minutes before serving.

SERVES 6

CHAPTER 34

Sheer delight

I sat at the computer putting photos together and looking back on the last three years, reflecting on the happy experience of reaching another milestone. I turned sixty and had the good fortune to celebrate it with close friends in a much-loved place. We were fortunate enough to be in Saignon again, Kiwis flying north for a few weeks of warmth after a mean winter. A loose invite to friends was circulated in the New Zealand summer. 'How about coming to France and meeting us there next August/September?' By late March four couples were committed and by mid-winter the number had grown to twelve people. In the end, although we all had a connection with New Zealand, we were coming together from around the globe. There were houses to rent in Saignon and timetables to make. I emailed my friend Kamila in Saignon, whom I knew to be a good cook.

'Dear Kamila, how would you feel about cooking for me for my birthday?'

Numerous emails later, Kamila said she and her daughter Nora would make a 'petite fête' for me. What menu would I like, how many, what date, etc. In the depths of a New Zealand winter it was exciting to be planning delicious meals for late summer in France!

Kamila and her artist husband Pierre are also the owners and hosts of a unique and delightful accommodation in Saignon, providing both apartments for longer-term stays and rooms for individual or short-term stays. They would accommodate our overflow.

And so it happened, the petite fête. Here is my diary entry from the morning after:

Je suis en septieme ciel! (I am in 7th Heaven!)

In the softness of early morning, 10 September, I am remembering my sixtieth birthday celebration before the immediacy of the experience fades. The menu cards hand-made for each guest by Pierre, Kamila's husband, were each an artistic delight.

The starter—Gazpacho—the freshness of Provençal tomatoes and a tiny surprise in the bottom of the glass (a piece of feta cheese). The glass placed on top of a fig leaf on the plate—a sharp contrast of red, green and white.

Entrée—Buffalo mozarella with lemon zest and pimento. A clear fresh dish, the perfection of colour on the plate—white, yellow, green—finely cut green pepper topped with two pieces of hot bright red pimento strips.

Then petite flan de aubergine—really another entrée—a flan sitting in a bed of red pepper puree. Tiny, delicate, delicious.

The plat—the main—lapin confit aux herbes de Provence avec une puree de pommes de terres et courgette a l'huile d'olive de St Saturnin. Which means rabbit—loins for the men and legs and thighs for the ladies, beautifully presented on a bed of courgette grated finely with potato with olive oil from nearby St Saturnin.

The rabbit is garnished with slivers of sliced summer truffle, gorgeous to taste, and to me, much nicer than the stronger winter truffle. This thought is not shared by all at the table. The rabbit had been sitting in a marinade for 24 hours, with thick bunches of herbs—thyme and marjoram—*and* has an intoxicating aroma. The next day the marinade was drained off and the herbs thrown away. For the final cooking, fresh marjoram is added for flavour. The rabbit is browned on the top of the gas oven and then baked in the oven in a heavy-lidded iron pot, long and slow.

The cheeses were divine and the wines were perfect, selected with assistance from Kamila. A small chevre from just down the road, a Pyrenees vache, Livareaux and a St Felicien brie. We failed to do justice to these cheeses, or the delicious breads from a specialty shop in Apt, shaped and stuffed with black olives.

Lastly the dessert, the St Tropez vanille crème gateau tropezienne, as described on the menu card, its presentation superb with pale pink rose buds surrounding the plate and decorating the top. It was a gorgeous cake, not too sweet. Everyone was very happy, especially me.

There we were, all far from home, being served an exquisite meal surrounded by celebratory decorations suggestive, as Kamila said, of Bacchus. There were pumpkins, rosemary and the last of the lavender in huge swaths inside the fireplace. On the table there were grape leaves and bunches of tiny black grapes. The table napkins were beautifully folded fans and the carte de menu rolled and tied with green raffia. The light from the candles was perfect, and the table shape—Kamila insisted on a semi circle—worked exactly as she said it would, making conversation between diners easier. It also gave her and her helper, Netege, easy access for serving. Their service was impeccable. There was no music, just the sound of late summer crickets outside as the night turned velvety.

When we had to leave it was hard to say goodbye, the parting sad. I didn't want to surrender it all, the peace, the pastel colours, the simple whitewashed walls of our rented house, the church bell ringing on the hour for the village and surrounding district, the cobbled streets, the old man and his dog opposite the pâtisserie. One last glimpse of Pierre and Kamila waving, their golden Labrador sitting on the stone outside the door, the whole scene framed by plane trees.

It was slightly dusty everywhere after the long hot summer, as they awaited the autumn rain. The roofers on a house nearby were replacing the tiles in preparation for the cold winter ahead as we were dispersing, each of us heading back to our other worlds.

Looking from the kitchen window to the north I saw the half moon hanging brightly in the early night sky. I was back in the southern hemisphere. The moon was hanging the wrong way round—this strange reversal phenomenon continues to fascinate me. The birds' chattering increases in volume and, with its perfect clarity, the call of a bellbird rose as soft mists began to lift from the lower hills of Banks Peninsula.

The indulgence of travel and eating is wonderful. But it is everyday rhythms and routines and the company of family and friends that give life its meaning and value. So, it is at home, sharing dinner with good friends under the grape arbour, white muslin curtains framing the outdoor eating space, we toasted in the New Year and nibbled on whitebait simply dusted with flour and quick-fried on the grill, accompanied by wedges of lemon and ribbons of fresh baby courgettes. We followed this standout starter with barbecued chicken breasts infused with chopped rosemary, olive oil and lemon zest and tiny new potatoes—my favourite Pentland dells—straight from the garden.

Crispy green beans and roasted red peppers with a splash of balsamic completed the main plate. And then to a green salad of buttercrunch lettuce, fresh from the garden. The meal completed, as the light began to fade, with fresh raspberries and a scoop of home-made ginger ice cream.

Grilled whitebait with lemony courgette ribbons

This dish is very fast to cook and must be eaten straightaway. If you don't have courgettes, the whitebait are a delicious appetiser on their own.

½ cup plain flour
salt and pepper
400g whitebait, drained and patted dry with paper towel
6 small courgettes
lemon zest
2 tbspn lemon juice
5 tbspn extra virgin olive oil

1 Sprinkle the flour, salt and pepper on a chopping board and lightly toss the whitebait on the board so each individual whitebait is coated.
2 Using a large peeler or mandolin cutter, shave the courgettes into long ribbons.
3 Place in a bowl with the lemon zest and juice and half the olive oil. Allow to sit at room temperature for 2 to 3 hours.
4 Arrange the courgette ribbons on the serving platter in curls.
5 Heat the grill to a very high temperature with a little bit of oil.
6 Drop the whitebait in batches onto the very hot grill plate, taking care to keep them separated.
7 As each batch is cooked, remove and serve immediately.

SERVES 6 AS AN APPETISER

Barbecued chicken breasts infused with rosemary, olive oil and lemon zest

The chicken cooked in this way is always tender and tasty. A very simple dish to prepare, these parcels can be cooked with equal success in the oven

4–6 chicken breasts
olive oil
zest of 1 lemon
fresh rosemary, finely chopped
salt and pepper to taste

1 Place each chicken breast onto a piece of tinfoil.
2 In a bowl, mix the oil, lemon zest and chopped rosemary.
3 Pour some of this mixture over each of the chicken breasts and season with salt and pepper. Bring the tinfoil up around the chicken and make into secure packages so no liquid can escape as they cook.
4 Place on the barbecue and cook for about 30 minutes (if cooking in the oven, place all packages together in an ovenproof dish in the oven at 200°C for about 20 minutes), until the chicken is cooked through. To serve, tip the chicken breast from the package and cut into thick slices. Arrange the slices on the plates and pour the juices over the meat.

SERVES 6–8

Stewed red peppers

An essential accompaniment to many meals, this perfect pepper dish brings colour and wonderful flavours to the plate. Serve hot or cold, with a main course or as a dish on its own.

7–8 tbspn olive oil
2 large onions, sliced
4 juicy fat peppers, deseeded and cut into wide strips
300g fresh ripe tomatoes, seeded and quartered, or 1 × 400g can chopped
*   tomatoes*
½ tspn tomato paste
salt
3 tbspn red wine vinegar
75g green olives

1 Preheat the oven to 180°C.
2 Heat half the oil in a heavy-based frying pan and fry the onions until just soft. Set aside.
3 Add the remainder of the oil and the peppers to the pan and fry until the peppers begin to seal and then add the onion, tomatoes and tomato paste.
4 Stir and season with salt.
5 Sprinkle in the vinegar and add the olives.
6 Stir well, then cook in a lidded dish for 30 to 40 minutes until the peppers are just cooked but not mushy.

SERVES 4–6

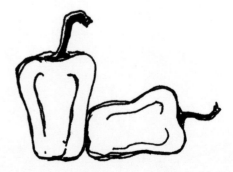

Ginger ice cream

This is my favourite ice cream and it's a superb accompaniment to poached peaches or pears.

2 eggs, separated
½ cup sugar
1 tspn warm water
2 drops vanilla essence
300ml whipping cream
150g stem ginger in heavy syrup, pureed (add a little of the syrup when
  pureeing the ginger)

1 Put the egg whites in a medium-sized bowl and beat until peaks form.
2 Add half the sugar and beat again until stiff.
3 Put the warm water in with the egg yolks and beat until frothy.
4 Add the remaining sugar and beat until pale and thick.
5 Add the vanilla.
6 Whip the cream to soft peaks and gently fold the beaten egg whites, yolks and ginger into the cream.
7 Freeze until firm.

SERVES 6–8

CHAPTER 35

When all else fails, cook

Life can be tough, and circumstances can change abruptly and not always for the best. Sometimes we feel like giving up. The things we used to celebrate, the energy we had for joyous events, are hard to activate. What has kept me going through challenging times is cooking every day for our household and extended family.

The economy has been challenging. My old shopping habits have had to change, but we all still need to be fed. Halcyon days in Provence and Governors Bay summers seem far away in the depths of a bad Christchurch winter. When there are unwanted dramas on every front—family, friends, business and health—everything can look and feel grey and glum, and not do-able.

Our accountant presents me with a gift. Not the usual cheer up or rewards of chocolate fish as is her habit, but a cookbook called *Sausages and Mince*. 'Now don't turn up your nose,' she announces, 'it's sausages and mince time.'

I proudly tell her sausages have been on the menu a lot this year, but receive the book graciously. I quietly add the sausages have to be good, and the ones I buy are *very* good. I've had a favourite recipe for sausage ragoût for a long time. It's a great winter cheer-up dish and makes an excellent lunch for the office next day. Yes, lunches for the office for our forestry business have become a regular feature. Reports from the office are that those on the receiving end feel excited by their lunches, are able to work more effectively and, of course, the cost is minimal compared to going out to buy lunch. A new office and the acquisition of a kitchen has changed all our eating habits. I find it quite easy to save part of the evening meal and box it for the next day's office lunch.

So yes, the world economic recession is making its presence felt, even here in New Zealand. I don't like having my pantry down on its usual wide selection of ingredients but the years during the 1970s and 80s have left a repertoire of survival skills in the kitchen that are being put to good use again. The darkest of days are brightened by a stoical determination to produce delicious food.

Then we had the first of the Christchurch earthquakes, and everything suddenly became a whole lot tougher as we all had to cope with a large-scale natural disaster.

On Sunday, 4 September 2010, I received a very different sort of birthday when, at 4.35 am, a 7.1 magnitude earthquake changed life in Canterbury forever. Our city, Christchurch, was badly injured. We were expecting to have three grandchildren sleeping with us that weekend and, with not much in the way of food in the house on Friday night, we planned to go to the market on Saturday morning.

We're often told to be ready for emergencies, to have water, canned food, torches, batteries, a transistor radio etc. on hand. The Governors Bay community is a resilient lot, used to severe weather conditions, power cuts and water and sewerage problems. But this event was so devastating that it took away our usual energy for coping and replaced it with fear. It was hard to think straight, to plan your day, feed your family or even yourself, with such a high level of uncertainty.

The initial terrifying quake was one thing, but it was the aftershocks that had exhausted and unnerved so many of us. But even with the ground wobbling like an angry beast, people need to be fed, homes need to regain some semblance of order. Food supplies have to be found and the appetites of traumatised little people need to be coaxed.

Since that first big shake, we craved comfort food and old English classics made a return, with an Indian addition. Split peas and canned tomatoes were in good supply in my pantry, and the usual variety of spices, so I began cooking dahl. When the butcher reopened some days later there were ham bones, and pea and ham soup emerged from my kitchen. Now, I keep a ham hock in the freezer at all times—just in case!

Pea and ham soup

This extremely comforting and nourishing soup saw us through many dark nights after the quakes.

1½ cups dried green split peas, soaked overnight, drained and rinsed
1 onion, chopped
1 carrot, chopped
1 celery stalk, chopped
2 bay leaves
1 ham hock
½ cup frozen peas, blanched
salt and pepper
crusty bread, to serve

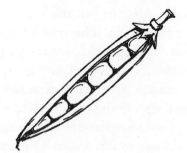

1 Place the split peas, onion, carrot, celery, bay leaves and ham hock into a pan.

2 Add enough water to cover and bring to the boil. Continue simmering over a low heat for 1½ hours, stirring occasionally, until the peas start to break down and the meat on the hock is tender.

3 Discard the bay leaves.

4 Remove the hock and set aside.

5 Allow the soup and hock to cool slightly.

6 Remove the ham from the hock and chop, discarding the skin and bone.

7 Blend the soup ingredients, in batches, finally adding the ham. Continue to blend until the soup is smooth.

8 To serve, return the soup to a saucepan, add the peas and bring to the boil. Season to taste with salt and pepper and serve piping hot with the bread.

SERVES 6

The chickens kept on laying throughout the major quake and the months of aftershocks, so eggs featured prominently. A favourite dessert resurrected from the past was baked egg custard.

I used mince—pork and beef—to make tasty meatballs to tempt nervous eaters. The grandchildren were enthusiastic. We took some of them to the spa town of Hanmer as a respite from the aftershocks and I made large quantities of pork and coriander meatballs, which they drenched in tamari and soy sauce. They are a high-energy snack before walks and dips in the hot pools.

I used beef mince for a tomato meatball dish and even I was enthused—the taste was light and fresh from generous additions of rosemary and parsley. After the quick browning of the patties came long slow cooking in the tomato passata, which had been prepared separately. This makes a wonderful meal with lightly grilled ciabatta or sourdough bread, or accompanied by mash or pasta. It's a real hit with the whole family. Later, one of our sons opens a sandwich bar and one of the favourites turns out to be spicy meatball sandwiches based on this dish.

Post-earthquake we felt like huddling in groups for comfort, to share a meal. So much energy was taken up daily, bracing against the aftershocks, our bodies constantly on high alert, that energy-rich meals were essential. None of us felt much like standing in the kitchen preparing food, never knowing when the next rattle, shake and bang was coming.

I'd had to leave my kitchen to climb under the oak dining table many times since the first earthquake, always worried about whether the gas would be on with food cooking at the time of a shake. During the first three days after each major quake we were without power. Luckily, we were able to use the wood stove for cooking. The soups and stews were delicious after the first big one, because it was still early spring, but the second quake came in late summer, so we barbecued meat and made pasta sauces.

Shared meals have been hugely important for keeping our spirits up. One night that Spring, with my husband away, I invited my friend Jan to stay the night. Making my way home via the obligatory detours, I tried not to get the directions wrong in congested traffic. Amidst all the signs saying 'Have moved to . . .', 'Closed' and 'Merge like a zip', I saw one saying 'Whitebait for sale'. The opening of the whitebait season had gone unnoticed in all the post-earthquake confusion.

I turned off and followed the sign, which led me to a fish shop I hadn't been to before. It felt disloyal, but like the cheesemonger my usual fish provider had gone, his building demolished. The tenacity of small business owners is remarkable. Restaurants were hard hit with some favourites no longer operable. With collapsed buildings or buildings deemed too dangerous, it must have been overwhelming for these people to see their hard work in ruins. Once again I was reminded that the underlying chaos and grief post-earthquake isn't as visible as the spectacle of broken buildings.

So Jan and I would have a treat—fresh whitebait followed by spicy fish and pumpkin soup.

Whitebait Mount Cook style

45g wild rice
20g basmati rice
2 eggs, separated
20g softened butter
125g whitebait
2g fresh coriander
salt and pepper, to taste

1 Set the oven to 180°C. Butter and flour two oval 10-12cm ramekins.
2 Cook the rices until soft, drain and set aside to cool.
3 Whisk the egg whites until soft and foamy.
4 In a separate bowl, beat the butter and egg yolks and combine with the rice, whitebait and coriander.
5 Fold in the egg whites and season with pepper and salt.
6 Put the mixture into each prepared ramekin filling to the top.
7 Bake for 9 minutes or until puffed up.
8 Remove from the oven and rest for 5 minutes before unmoulding.

SERVES 2

Spicy fish and pumpkin soup

I like to use monkfish cod or snapper for this comforting meal in a bowl.

2 tbspn olive or canola oil
4 shallots, thinly sliced
1 small sweet red pepper, deseeded and thinly sliced
1 small sweet yellow pepper, deseeded and thinly sliced
1 green pepper, deseeded and cut into strips
1 tbspn red curry paste (optional)
200ml light coconut milk or coconut cream
3 cups chicken stock
2 kaffir lime leaves, finely shredded (optional)
250g pumpkin, peeled and cut into 2cm pieces
1 tspn tamarind paste
2 tbspn fish sauce
1 tbspn brown sugar
salt
600g skinless chunky fish fillets, cut into 3cm pieces
100g baby spinach leaves, washed and stalks removed

1   Heat the oil in a heavy-based deep frying pan over medium–high heat.
2   Add the shallots and the peppers and sear for about 2 minutes.
3   If using curry paste add it now and cook, stirring, for 2 minutes or until fragrant.
4   Add the coconut milk, stock and kaffir lime leaves, if using. Stir to combine.
5   Add the pumpkin, tamarind, fish sauce, sugar and a pinch of salt and cook for 20 minutes or until the pumpkin is tender.
6   Finally add the pieces of fish and simmer for 5 minutes or until the fish is opaque.

7 To serve, divide the prepared spinach between two warmed serving
  bowls and top with the fish and vegetable soup.

SERVES 2

As we were relaxing and sitting down to eat, a reasonable-sized
aftershock hit. I was about to cry as I realised we had another night
of shaking and uncertainty ahead. As the shake passed, I downed
a glass of chardonnay and tried to eat. We were both exhausted,
so we decided to head upstairs to bed to watch TV, hoping that
would be a distraction. We climbed in together and tried to watch
TV and after an hour or so of calm, we began to feel confident
we might be in for a better night so we bid each other goodnight
and Jan made her way to bed in my office. 'Goodnight,' we called,
lights out, heads down.

Then the dressing table began to wobble and it was a big one
that unnerved us both. I wished I hadn't put everything back on
it during the day as I wondered just how big the shakes would
get. We survived the night but it wasn't easy.

By October the rhododendrons and azaleas were in full bloom,
and the deep-purple iris was beginning to show. Family and friends
gathered here at Ribbonwood to celebrate spring and resilience—it's
our thanksgiving for surviving the quakes. There were ten adults
and eight children. We ate outside, the first long-table outdoor
eating of the season. Outdoor furniture had been retrieved from
the sheds and the umbrella put up. People served themselves
from the small outdoor table then picked up their cutlery and
napkins from the box where I'd placed them, making the serving
stress-free for me.

Children served their own meal and ate where they liked in the garden. They ran wild, celebrating freedom from winter, earthquakes and the watchful eyes of parents, as they disappeared into the rambling walkways.

The menu reflected a celebration—it's tasty simplicity, but this time it was also low cost. I provided pitchers of iced water, a large dish of meatballs in spicy tomato sauce, two loaves of rosemary flat bread, baked just before the guests arrived, two bowls of salad greens fresh from the garden and a platter of barbecued pork, apple and sage sausages. The eight-year-old girls had three helpings of meatballs each and the adults enjoyed chardonnay and pinot gris.

Delicious meatballs in tomato sauce

For the meatballs
2 cloves garlic, chopped, plus 1 clove, halved
4 slices pancetta or streaky bacon
1 cup sourdough breadcrumbs
2 tspn chopped rosemary
¼ cup chopped parsley, plus extra to serve
600g beef mince
2 tbspn tomato paste
1 egg

For the sauce
2 tbspn olive oil
250g punnet cherry tomatoes, halved or 1 × 400g can cherry tomatoes

1 tspn brown sugar
2 tspn red wine vinegar
3 cups tomato purée
grated parmesan

1 To make the meatballs, place the chopped garlic in a processor with the pancetta, breadcrumbs, rosemary and parsley and pulse until finely chopped.
2 Place in a bowl with the mince, tomato paste and egg and mix well with your hands.
3 Roll into 3cm balls and chill for 30 minutes. (It makes about 24 meatballs.)
4 Preheat the oven to 180°C.
5 To make the sauce, heat a little bit of the olive oil in a heavy-based frying pan and fry the tomatoes.
6 Add the sugar, red wine vinegar and purée and heat until the sugar has dissolved and a thick sauce has formed.
7 In another pan add some more of the olive oil and brown the meatballs in batches on both sides. You can flatten them a little at this point.
8 Place the browned meatballs in a baking dish and cover with the tomato sauce.
9 Cover with tinfoil and bake in a moderate oven for about 30 minutes.
10 To serve, sprinkle with freshly grated parmesan.

SERVES 6

Dessert was my version of tiramisu—as part of my ongoing economy drive it had no mascarpone. You would think this ingredient was vital but all voted the dessert a success. And then, to top it all off, I served a comforting rhubarb upside-down cake made with fresh rhubarb from the garden.

A sort of tiramisu

When you cannot get the mascarpone for whatever reason, this version of tiramisu is still very acceptable.

3 egg yolks
3 tbspn sugar
330ml marsala
225ml cream
1 egg white
60ml espresso coffee (or weaker coffee to reduce flavour)
125g Savoiardi biscuits (sponge fingers)

1 Beat the egg yolks and sugar in a bowl over a saucepan of simmering water and whisk until it becomes lighter in colour and thickens.
2 Add 80ml of the marsala and whisk again. Remove from the heat and set aside to cool.
3 Beat the cream until peaks form.
4 In a clean bowl, beat the egg white until stiff peaks form and blend the cream and egg whites together.
5 Mix the espresso with the remaining Marsala.
6 Dip half the Savoiardi biscuits in the liquor and arrange them in a single layer on the bottom of a bowl.
7 Cover them with half of the cream mixture.
8 Make another layer of dipped biscuits and top with the remaining cream.
9 Cover and place in the fridge until required.

SERVES 6

Rhubarb upside-down cake

This cake was the biggest hit during our first post-earthquake spring.

For the rhubarb
25g butter
25g caster sugar
3–4 rhubarb stems if large or up to 10 small ones, chopped
1 tbspn rosewater

For the syrup
150g caster sugar
150ml water
1 rhubarb stem, chopped
1 tbspn rosewater
juice of ½ a lemon

For the cake
100g butter
150g caster sugar
1 tspn vanilla
2 eggs, separated
150g flour
1½ tspn baking powder
125ml milk

1 To prepare the rhubarb, line the base of a 20cm springform tin with baking paper and grease with butter.
2 Gently heat the butter and caster sugar in a small saucepan until the mixture begins to caramelise.

3 Add the chopped rhubarb and stir over the heat for another minute, then pour the mixture into the prepared tin and set aside while you make the cake batter.

4 To make the syrup, heat the sugar and water in a small saucepan until the sugar dissolves and lastly add the rosewater.

5 Add the rhubarb and cook for 5 minutes.

6 Strain the mixture and add the rosewater and lemon juice to the syrup. Place the rhuburb in the prepared tin.

7 Preheat the oven to 180°C.

8 To make the batter, beat the butter and sugar together until pale and fluffy.

9 Add the vanilla then the egg yolks, one at a time, beating well after each addition.

10 Sieve the flour and baking powder and add to the egg in two lots, alternating with the milk.

11 Beat the egg whites to soft peaks then fold through the cake batter.

12 Spoon the batter on top of the rhubarb and smooth down, then bake for 50 minutes until the cake is firm to the touch.

13 Cool the cake for 5 minutes then run a knife around the sides of the tin and remove the side.

14 Invert the cake onto a serving plate, then carefully remove the base and baking paper.

15 Pour the strained syrup over the cake and serve warm with cream.

SERVES 6–8

Coffees and teas were poured and we relaxed in the hot sun. How terrible to think that just a few short months later, in February 2011, the most debilitating of the major quakes would strike, devastating Christchurch. As I write these lines in late 2013, quakes or no quakes life continues, and I reflect on the motivation of food preparation on a daily basis despite all that goes on in a full life. It constantly amazes me how I can go from having no idea what a meal is going to be, to creating one. The process interests me. How do I get myself from a state of disinterest to wanting to stay in and make a meal? Some discipline is involved, but mostly it is the reward of a pleasurable eating experience at home that gets me motivated. For me, the reward is greater than the effort. There is always a direct relationship between growing things and eating them, having hens on the property, feeding them and collecting their eggs, collecting the fruit and vegetables in order to create the food we eat. It's that simple.

Gastronomique, yes, for special occasions, but it's the simple meals using fresh and seasonal produce that bring colour and joy to our lives that should be celebrated, retained and passed on to the next generation. I have over recent years had the great pleasure of watching my now 15-year-old and 10-year-old granddaughters become passionate about cooking and growing things with younger ones watching on perhaps to follow.

As a cook in a temperate climate I'm attuned to seasonal cooking, adapting to what is available at different times of the year and using preparations that fit with the changing temperatures. My repertoire continues to grow—I'm always picking up ideas from others, from books, from magazines, from observations and tastings. I continue to be tempted to buy yet another cookbook and have the good fortune to be the recipient of many as gifts. And I'm never disappointed—there is always something new to inspire me, and another perspective to view.

How do you measure the value of years of treats at the table of a good friend? The cross fertilisation of ideas, the rescues from life's dramas with a delicious meal and conversation? How do you value knowing that when you arrive there will be order and an ambience created for your enjoyment, not to mention wonderful food? The good fortune of having a friend close by who enjoys the pleasures of food preparation and presentation has meant hundreds of meals shared and savoured. For me, this rates high on the measuring scale of life's pleasures.

The celebrations, the comfort of sharing with family and friends, of negotiating and sharing with business colleagues, the excitement of discovery while travelling, and the experimentation and daily providing back home—they are here . . . the lingering memories of those experiences, and some which bring just sheer delight. The recipes in this book have been gathered over the course of my life, although I unashamedly borrow and adapt and will be forever grateful to the many sources of my inspiration.

Basic essentials

There are some things that I always have on hand, either in the garden or in the pantry. With them, I am able to make nutritious and comforting meals every day with a minimum of fuss and in good time. I've listed them here for you.

Fresh free-range eggs—I know what my hens have been fed and the eggs look and taste different. Keeping hens guarantees us a steady supply of eggs for six to eight months of the year. And when you can get them fresh, duck eggs are a bonus.

Lemons—home-grown lemons. I prefer Meyer lemons for their thin skins and juiciness, and I find I can use them fresh in place of preserved lemons.

Fresh herbs—there's thyme, marjoram, parsley, sage and bay leaves available all year round, the summer annuals, especially basil and coriander, and perennials that reappear after each winter, including mint, fennel, tarragon and chives.

Vanilla—either a pure vanilla essence or vanilla beans. I use and re-use the beans, getting the very last bit of flavour from them. I wash and dry them after each use and store them in an airtight container until required.

Garlic—locally grown or at least New Zealand–grown garlic is essential.

Salt—Maldon sea salt is my first choice.

Peppercorns—black, pink and green if you can.

Jars of low-acid tomato purée

Good home-made chicken stock—there is always some in the freezer.

Good home-made beef stock—this is more time-consuming to make than chicken stock and I keep boxes of ready-made beef stock in the pantry.

Gelatine sheets

Oil—there is always a good quality olive oil and a good canola oil for cooking. I use extra virgin olive oil for dressings.

Quality aged balsamic vinegar—I find this is impossible to be without.

Canned beans and pulses—borlotti and cannellini beans, lentils and chickpeas. It is much easier than cooking the beans myself, especially when cooking for a small number of people.

Rice—there's a variety of rice in my pantry, each with its own flavour and virtues. Basmati has the longest grain, Camargue red rice is a cross between wild red rice and short-grain rice, arborio is a short-grain rice ideal for risotto and rice pudding, Calasparra is a short-grain perfect for paella, and wild rice is native to North America and has a high nutritional value.

Frozen peas

Tamari sauce

Fresh ginger root—if you don't use it very often keep it in the freezer.

Italian hard cheese such as grana padano or parmigiano reggiano—I keep the rinds in the freezer for flavouring soups.

Fresh fruit and vegetables—we have a selection of fruit trees and bushes in a smallish orchard space, including plums, apples, apricots, cherries, pears, quince, blackcurrants and redcurrants. We also have two quite small vege plots, but they give us a year-round supply of fresh produce. In summer we harvest courgettes, tomatoes, lettuce, new potatoes, beans and broccoli. In autumn we harvest tomatoes, pumpkins, spinach and cauliflower. In winter there are leeks, cabbages and some very hardy winter lettuce and rocket. These fresh tastes supplement our daily menu and keep us connected to the patterns of the seasons.

Home preserves and bottled sauces—when produce is in plentiful supply I make jellies, jams and sauces. Bottle fruit and freeze soups and fruit to keep on hand. They are a wonderful addition to everyday cooking.

Pancetta or good quality streaky bacon—there is always some in the freezer.

Rosie's reading list

Books

Alexander, Stephanie, *Cooking and Travelling in South-West France*, Camberwell, Victoria, Penguin, 2002.

Alexander, Victoria, Harris, Genevieve, *The Bathers Pavilion Cookbook*, Berkely, California, Ten Speed Press Ltd, 1995.

Allende, Isabel, *Aphrodite: A memoir of the senses*, New York, Harper Collins, 1998.

Amiard, Herve, Mouton, Laurence, Seguin-Tsouli, Maria, Rauzier, Maria-Pascal, *A Taste of Morocco Cuisine and Culture*, London, Hachette Illustrated, Octopus Publishing Group Ltd, 2001.

Andre, Jean-Louis, *Great French Chefs and their Recipes*, Paris, Editions Flammarion, 2003.

Arora, David, *Mushrooms Demystified*, Berkeley, Ten Speed Press, 1979.

Australian Gourmet Traveller Essentials, Sydney, ACP Publishing Pty Ltd, 2004.

Beck, Simone, Bertholle, Louisette, Child, Julia, *Mastering the Art of French Cooking Vol. 1*, London, Penguin, 1966.

Bosley, Martin, Martin Bosley *Auckland: Godwit*, Random House, 2010.

Buiso, Julie, *Never Ending Summer*, Auckland, New Holland, 2009.

Case, Frances, *1001 Foods You Must Taste Before You Die*, Universe, 2008.

Cooking French, Sydney, Murdoch Books Australia, 2006.

Cooper, Artemis, Writing at the Kitchen Table: Elizabeth David, the authorised biography, London, Penguin, 2000.

David, Elizabeth, *Elizabeth David Classics*, London, Grubb Street, 1999.

Espe Brown, Edward, *The Tassajara Bread Book*, San Francisco, Shambhala Publications Inc, 1970.

Gyngell, Skye, *A Year in My Kitchen*, London, Quadrille Publishing, 2006.

Mackay, Alex, *Cooking in Provence*, Great Britain, Headline Book Publishing, 2003.

Harris, Valentina, *Recipes from an Italian Farmhouse*, London, Conran Octopus, 1989.

Helstrom, Robert, *Contemporary Italian: Favourite recipes from Kulito's Italian restaurant*, California Union Square, 1993.

Holst, Simon and Alison, *Marvellous Mince & Sensational Sausages*, Amberley, Hyndman Publishing.

Leaf, Alexandra, Leeman, Fred, *Van Gough's Table*, New York, Artisan, 2001.

Le Clerc, Julie, *Made in Morocco*, Penguin.

Leibling, A.J., *Between Meals: An appetite for Paris*, New York, North Point Press, 1986.

Lippmann, Bernd, *Hermitage Cuisine Cookbook*, The Hermitage, Aoraki Mt Cook, 2002.

Lloyd, Christopher, *Gardener Cook*, London, Frances Lincoln Ltd, 1997.

Mahy, Margaret, *Jam*, Little Brown & Co, 1986.

McDonald, Margaret, *Whistler's Mother's Cookbook*, St Albans, Paul Elek Ltd, 1979.

Medici, Lorenzo de, *Italy The Beautiful Cookbook*, Frenchs Forest, Australia, Child & Associates Pty Ltd, 1998.

Moine, Marie –Pierre, *Cuisine Grand-Mere, Traditional French Home Cooking*, London, Ebury Press, 2001.

Painter, Gilian, *A New Zealand Country Harvest Cookbook*, Auckland, Random House, 1992.

Pretty, Ruth, *The Ruth Pretty Cookbook*, Auckland, Penguin, 2002.

Roberts, Deborah, de Montal, Victoire, *A Country Year in Gascony*, London, Ebury Press, 1990.

Scott, Sally Anne, *Recipes for a Country Weekend*, London, Conran Octopus Ltd, 1991.

Telford, Anthony, *The Kitchen Hand: A miscellany of kitchen wisdom*, Sydney, Allen & Unwin, 2003.

The New York Times Natural Foods Cookbook, Avon Books, 1971.

Wright, Simon, *The French Café Cookbook*, Auckland, Godwit (Random House), 2007.

Magazines

The Denizen
Cuisine
Harper's Bazaar
Mindfood
NZ House & Garden
Australian Gourmet Traveller
Australia Vogue Entertaining & Travel
Cote Sud
Dish

Index

Acknowledgements

The recipes and stories in this collection reflect a life lived to the full, sharing food with family and friends. For more than four decades, through all the events of our lives, my husband Mark has been my supportive companion. My thanks to children, Aimee, Mischa and Ollie, their partners, and my grandchildren Reuben, Sophia, Arlo, Lili, Grace and Iñaki for being my family around the table and to my mother and grandmother for the legacy of your influence.

To the production and editorial teams at Allen & Unwin in Auckland and Sydney, a huge thankyou for ushering this book into the world. Special thanks to Melanie Laville-Moore for your calm perseverance and encouragement, to Nic McCloy for your belief in me and my words, to Laura Mitchell for your amazing editorial guidance, Katy Yiakmis for the luscious cover design, Jo Rodwell for the quirky illustrations and to Fiona McRae who provided a long and detailed first edit. Miranda Van Asch was there at the beginning—thank you for giving the idea its start and for the years of valued friendship.

Thanks also to:

Lorain Day, for being the first reader, editing and adding more shape to my words and for your prompting me to 'get it out there.'.

Maria Cropper and Jeanette Stanley, for organising, typing, tasting, collating and deciphering my scrawl!

Sarah Lovell Smith, for continuing to inspire me with your wonderful cooking, and to Sarah and Philip King for the years of celebration of friendship and good eating experiences at each other's tables.

Robyn Belton, for being an early mentor. Your kitchens have remained spaces of warmth, conviviality and creativity.

Kim Hennessy, for your friendship and delight in the creations and ideas that come from my kitchen and Michelle Santana my enthusiastic apprentice, both of you encouraged me to share these recipes.

Alison Pearson, for all the years of food and ideas sharing, and Alan Pearson, with your love of life and honesty challenging me to be brave.

Kamila Regent – you taught me that perfection could be achieved; art and food made with love from a tiny kitchen in Saignon.

To the many wonderful people here and around the world with whom we have enjoyed friendship and food and to the restaurateurs, chefs and maître d's whose food and hospitality has excited and delighted me.

And to the late Margaret Mahy, whose continual enthusiasm, encouragement and friendship I cherish. I wish that you could be here to share in the publication of this work.